T0088449

CONNECT & COLOR

WORLD LANDMARKS

Copyright © 2016 by Racehorse Publishing

All rights reserved. No part of this book may be reproduced in any manner without the express written consent of the publisher, except in the case of brief excerpts in critical reviews or articles. All inquiries should be addressed to Racehorse Publishing, 307 West 36th Street, 11th Floor, New York, NY 10018.

Racehorse Publishing books may be purchased in bulk at special discounts for sales promotion, corporate gifts, fund-raising, or educational purposes. Special editions can also be created to specifications. For details, contact the Special Sales Department, Skyhorse Publishing, 307 West 36th Street, 11th Floor, New York, NY 10018 or info@skyhorsepublishing.com.

Racehorse Publishing™ is a pending trademark of Skyhorse Publishing, Inc.®, a Delaware corporation.

Visit our website at www.skyhorsepublishing.com.

10 9 8 7 6 5 4 3 2 1

Print ISBN: 978-1-944686-76-5

Printed in the United States of America

CONNECT & COLOR

WORLD LANDMARKS

AN INTRICATE COLORING AND DOT-TO-DOT BOOK

Racehorse Publishing

Dot-to-Dot Guide

◆ = Stop line here and look for next section

O = Begin new section

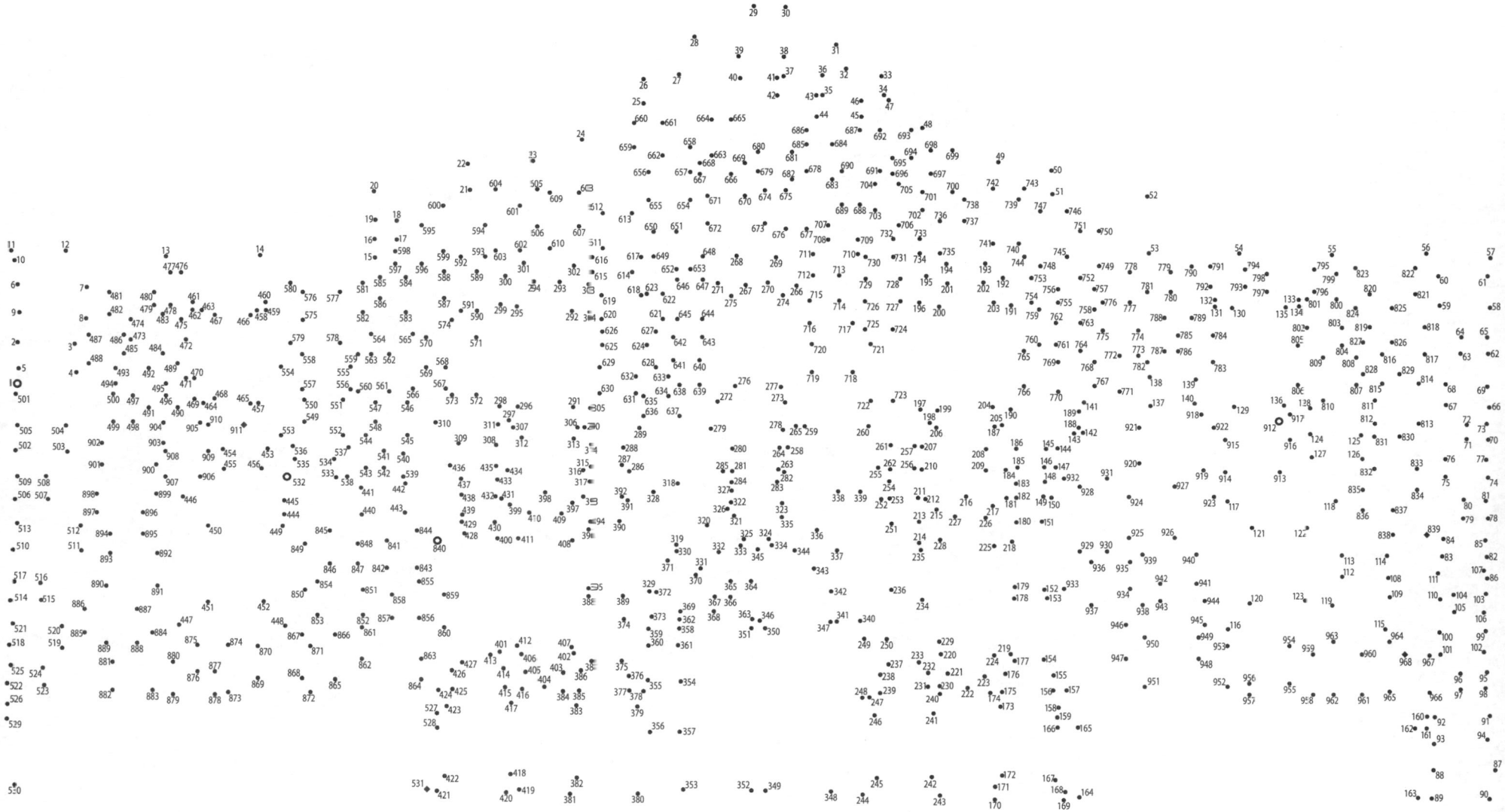

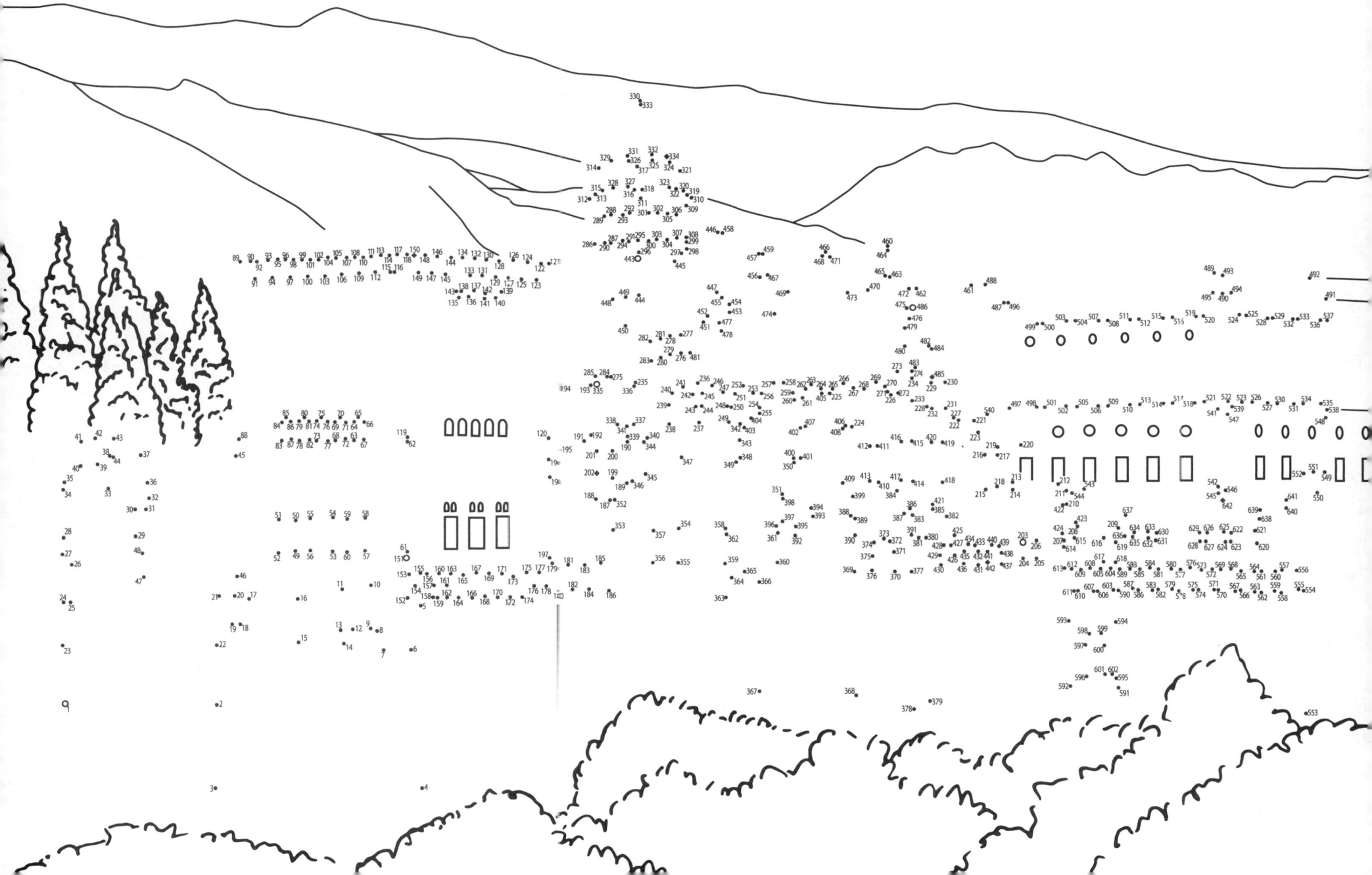

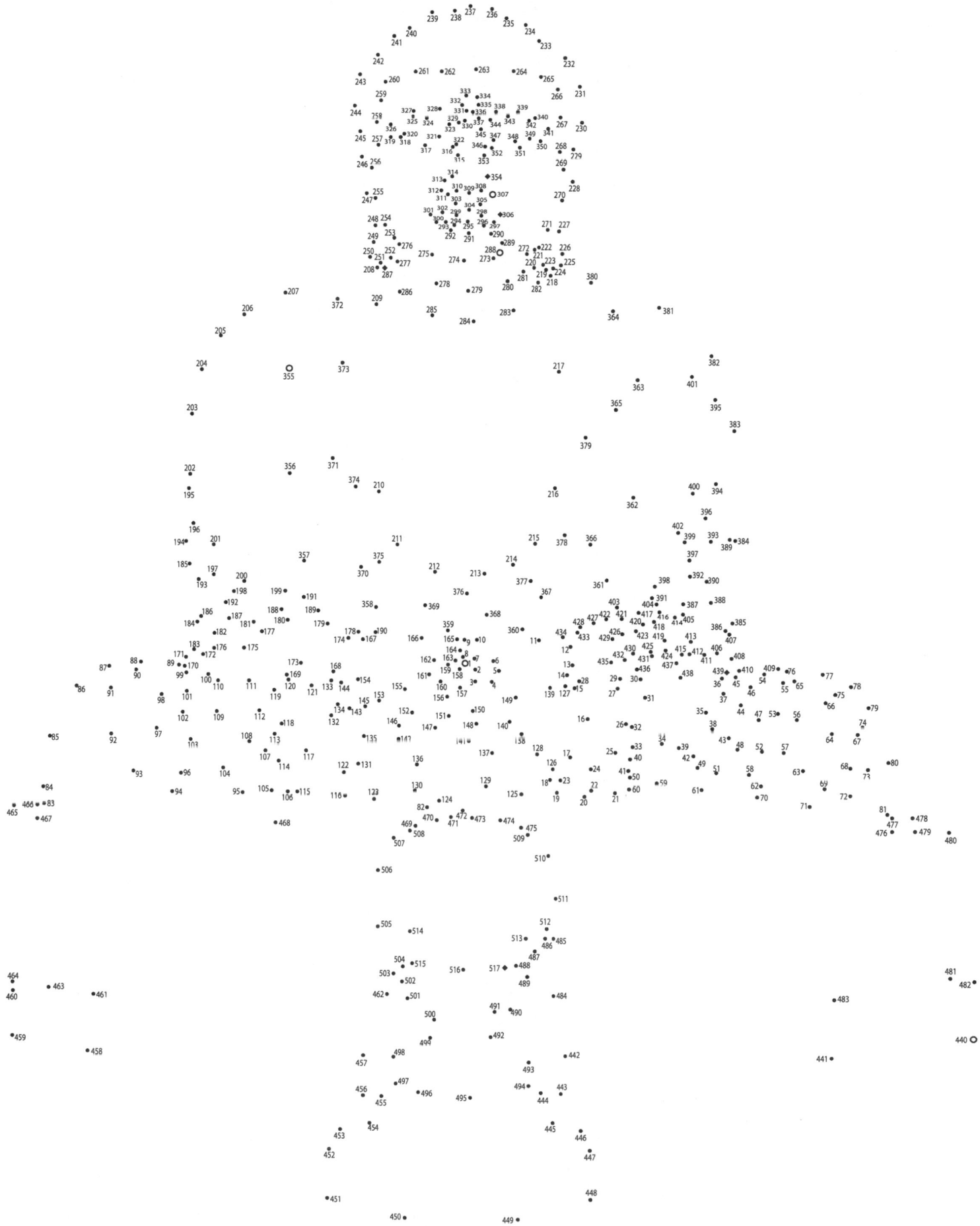

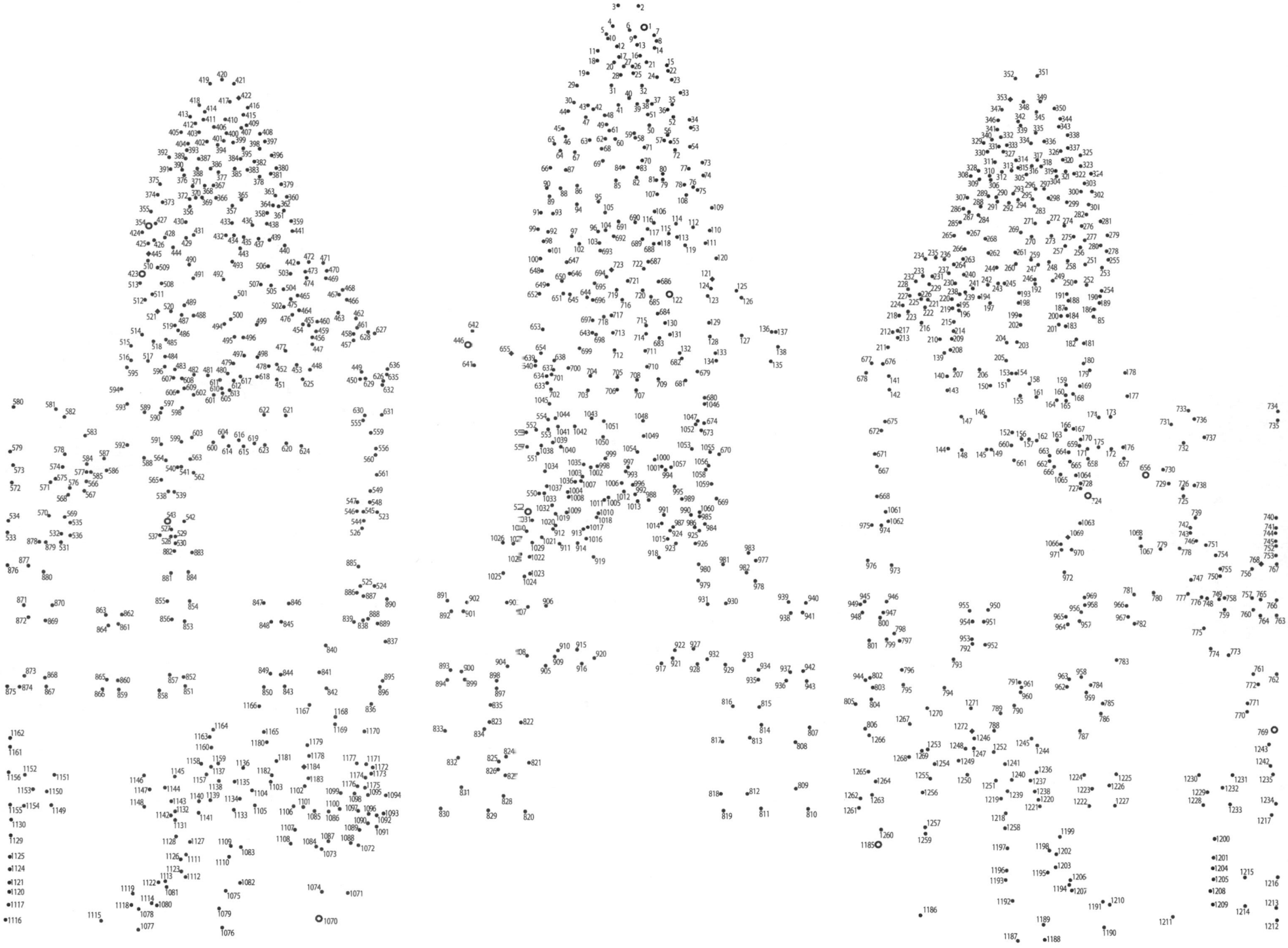

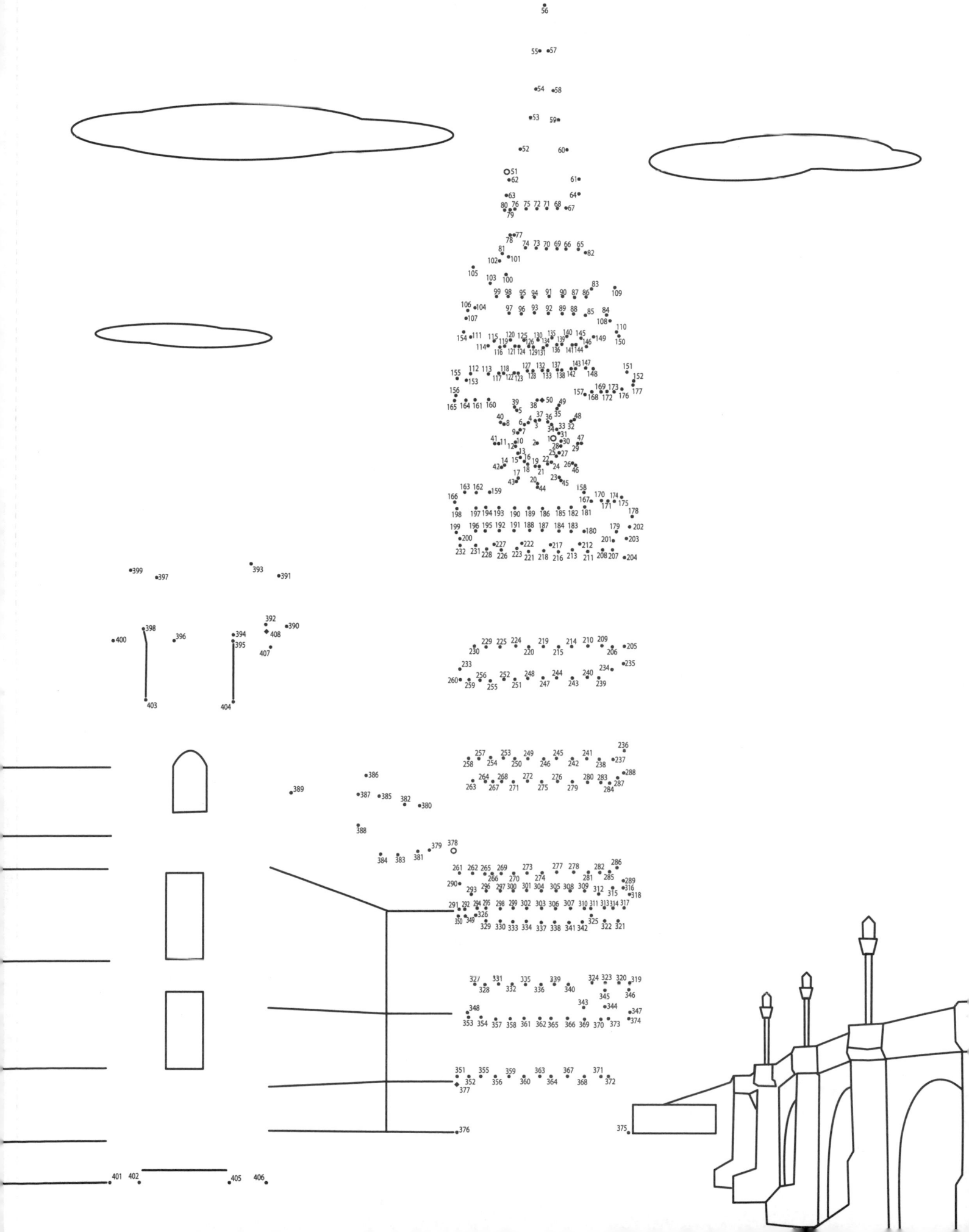

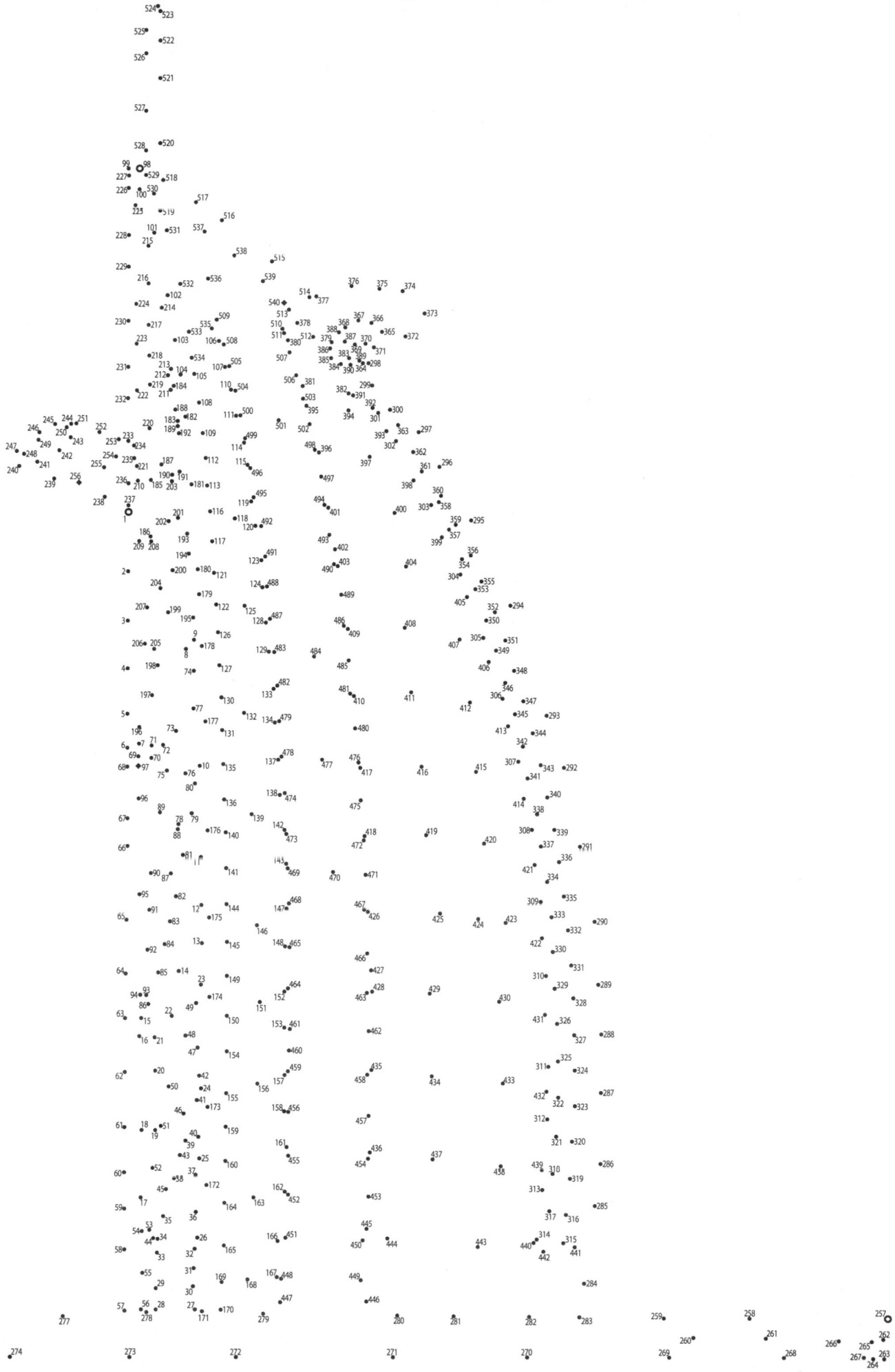

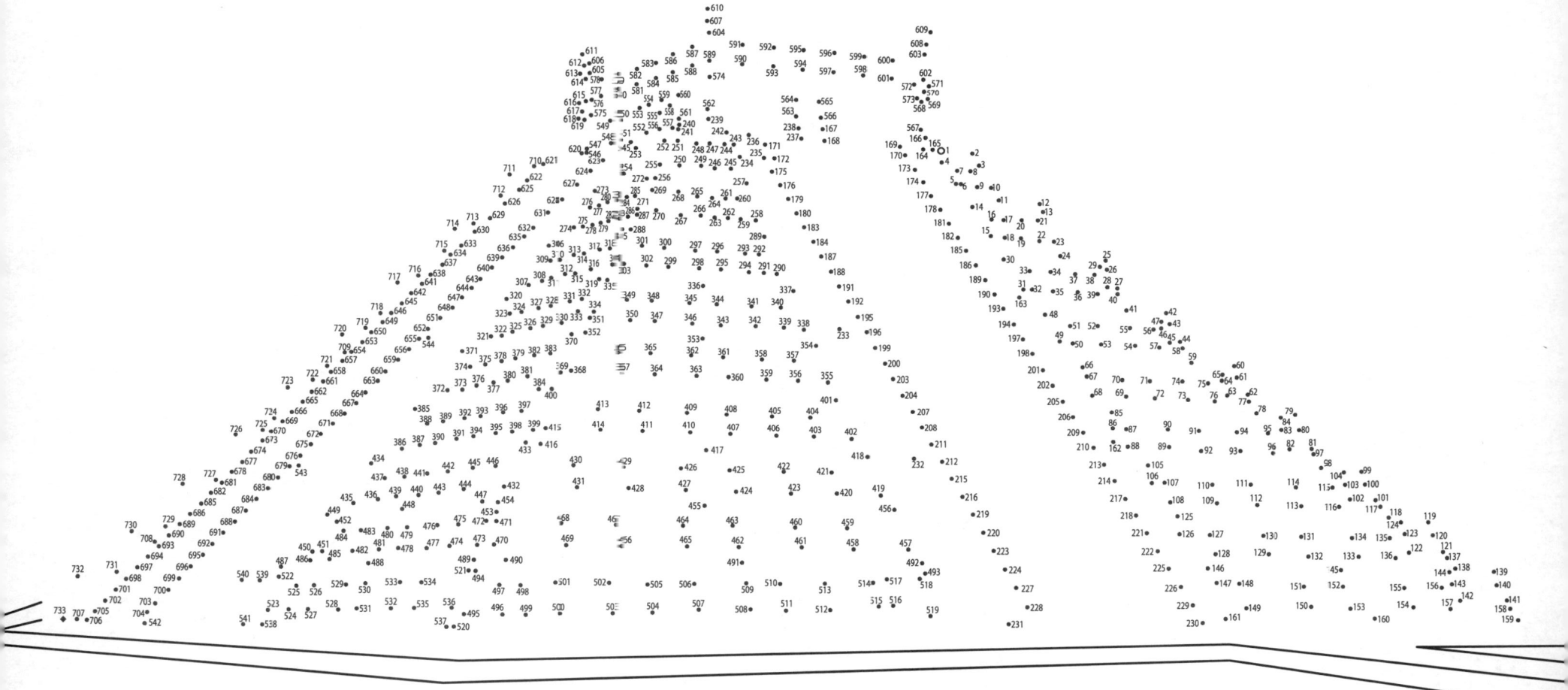

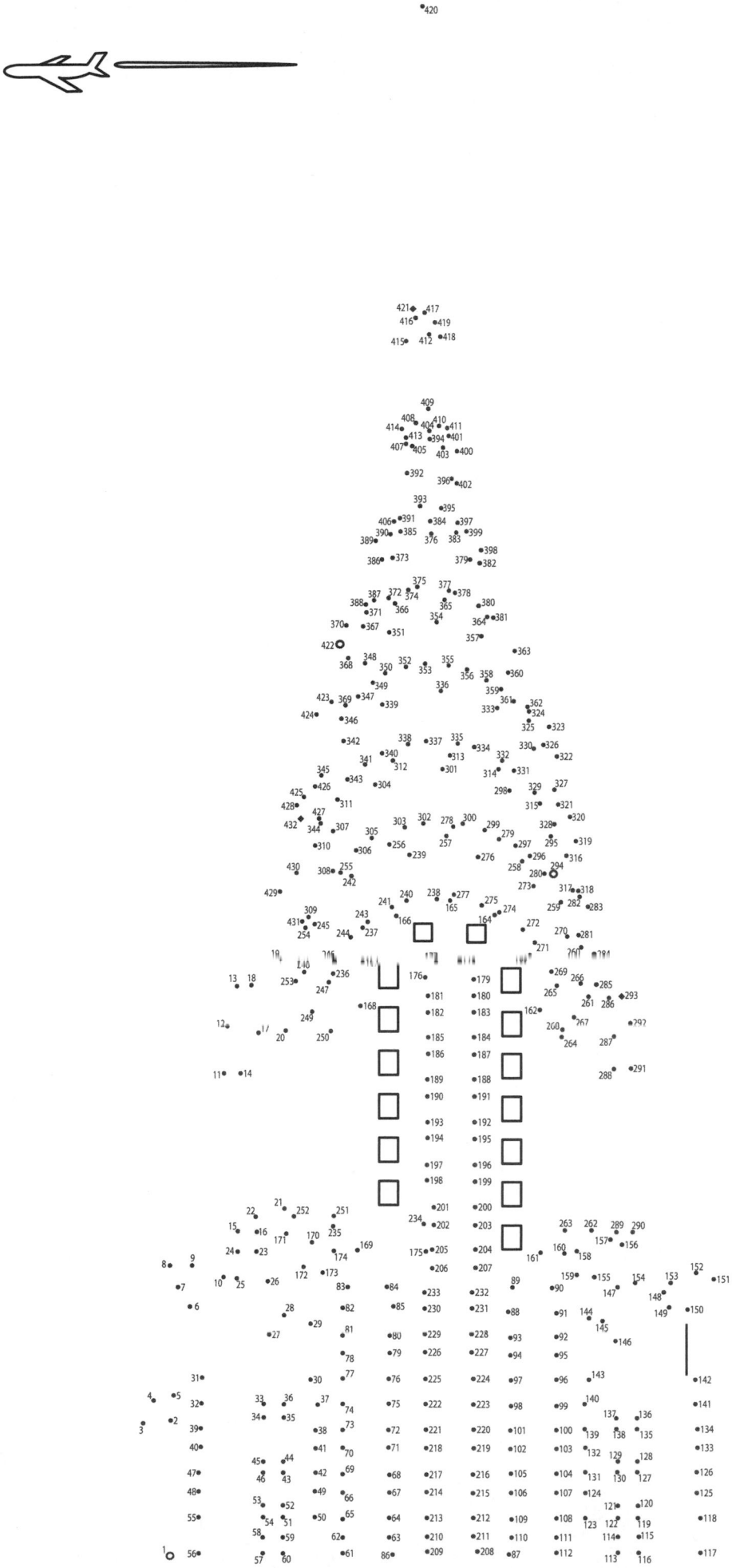

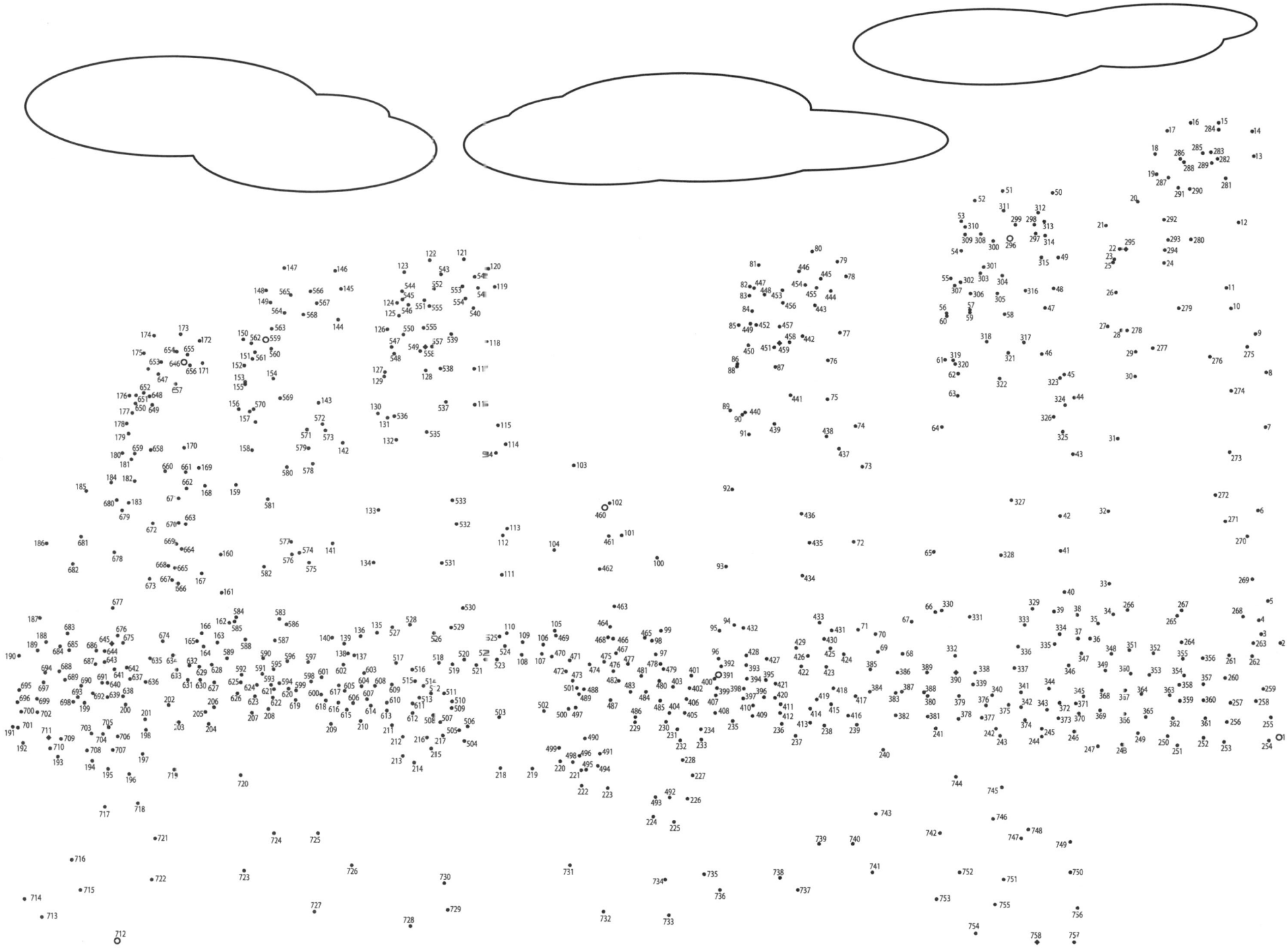

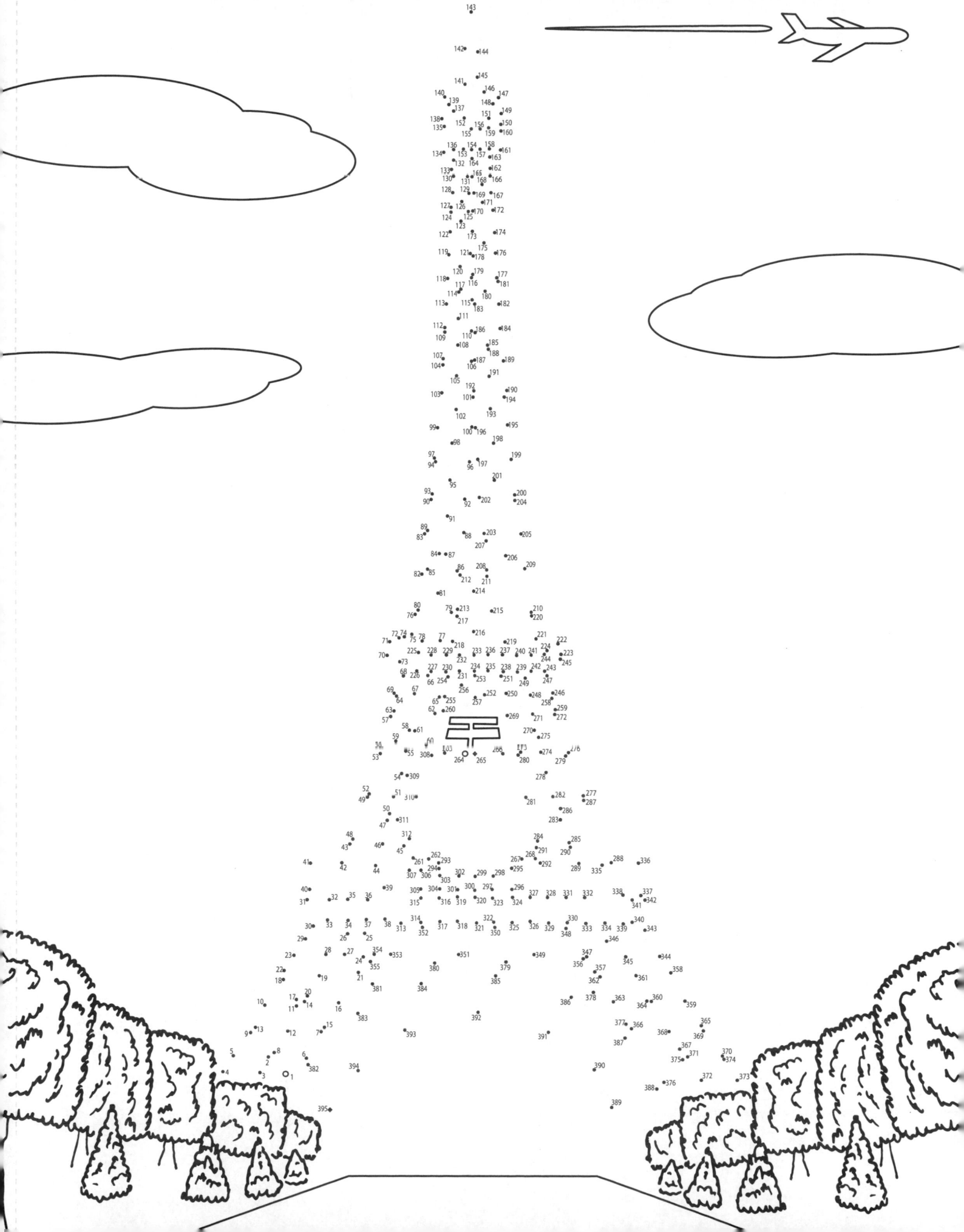

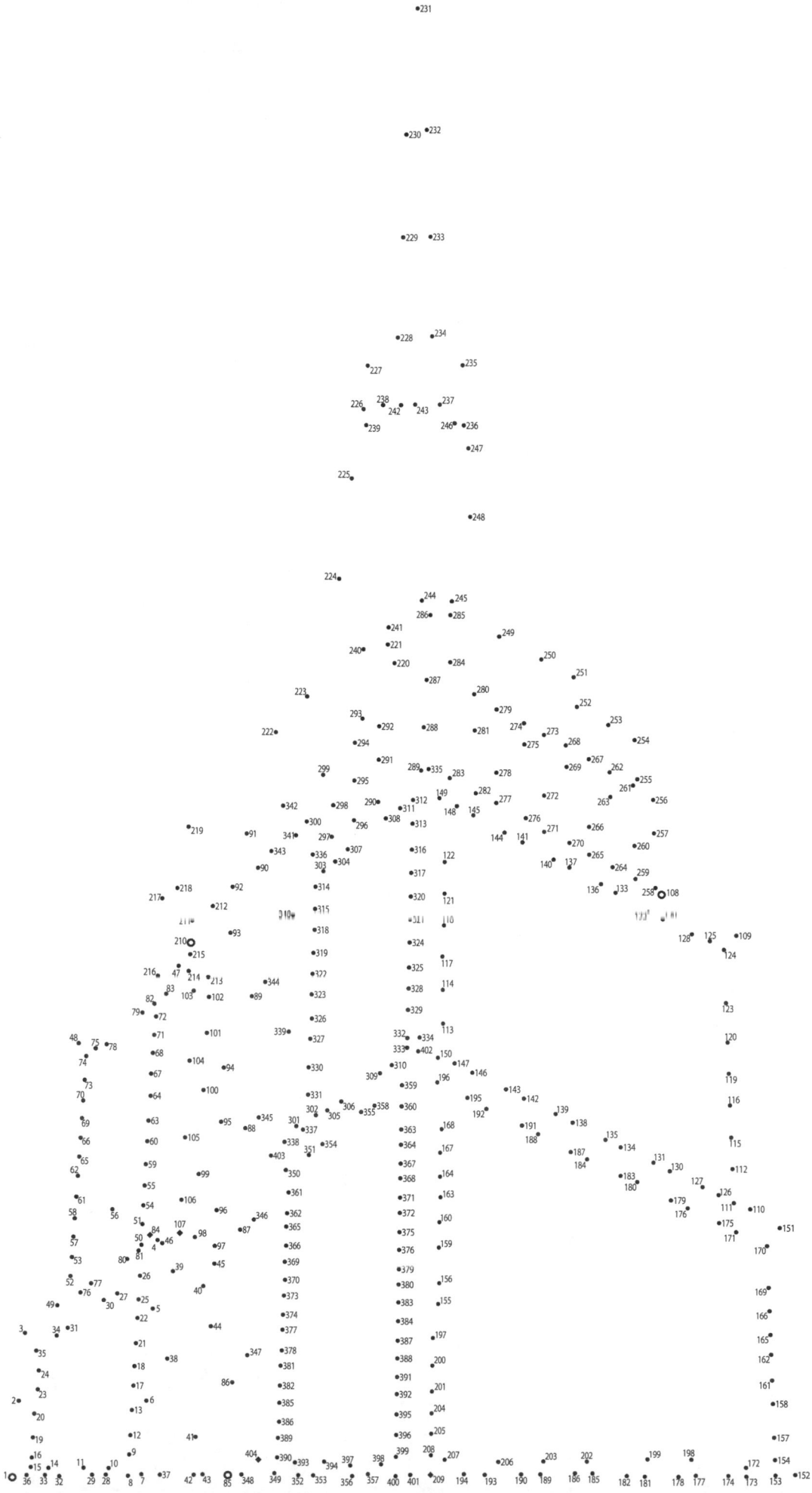

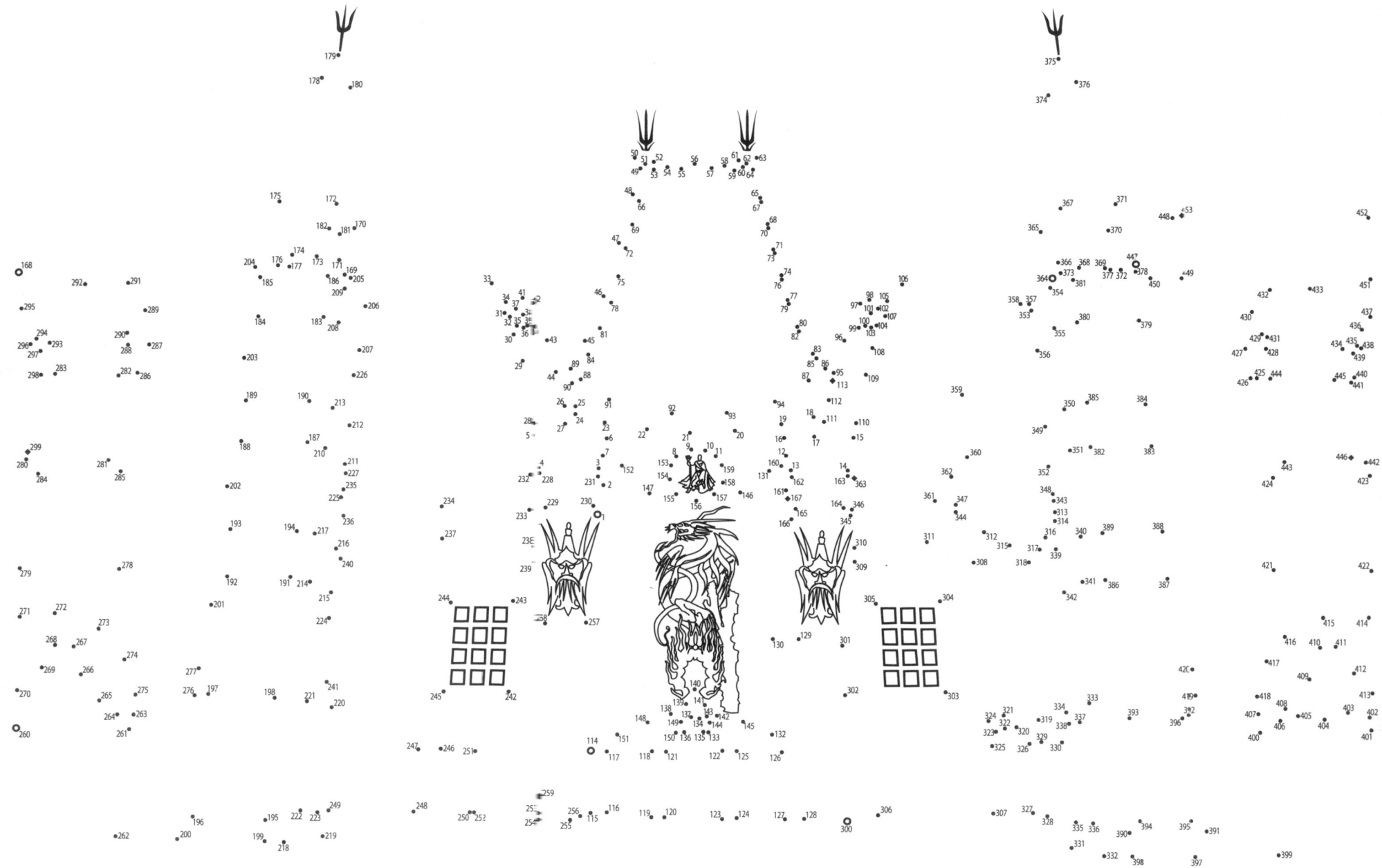

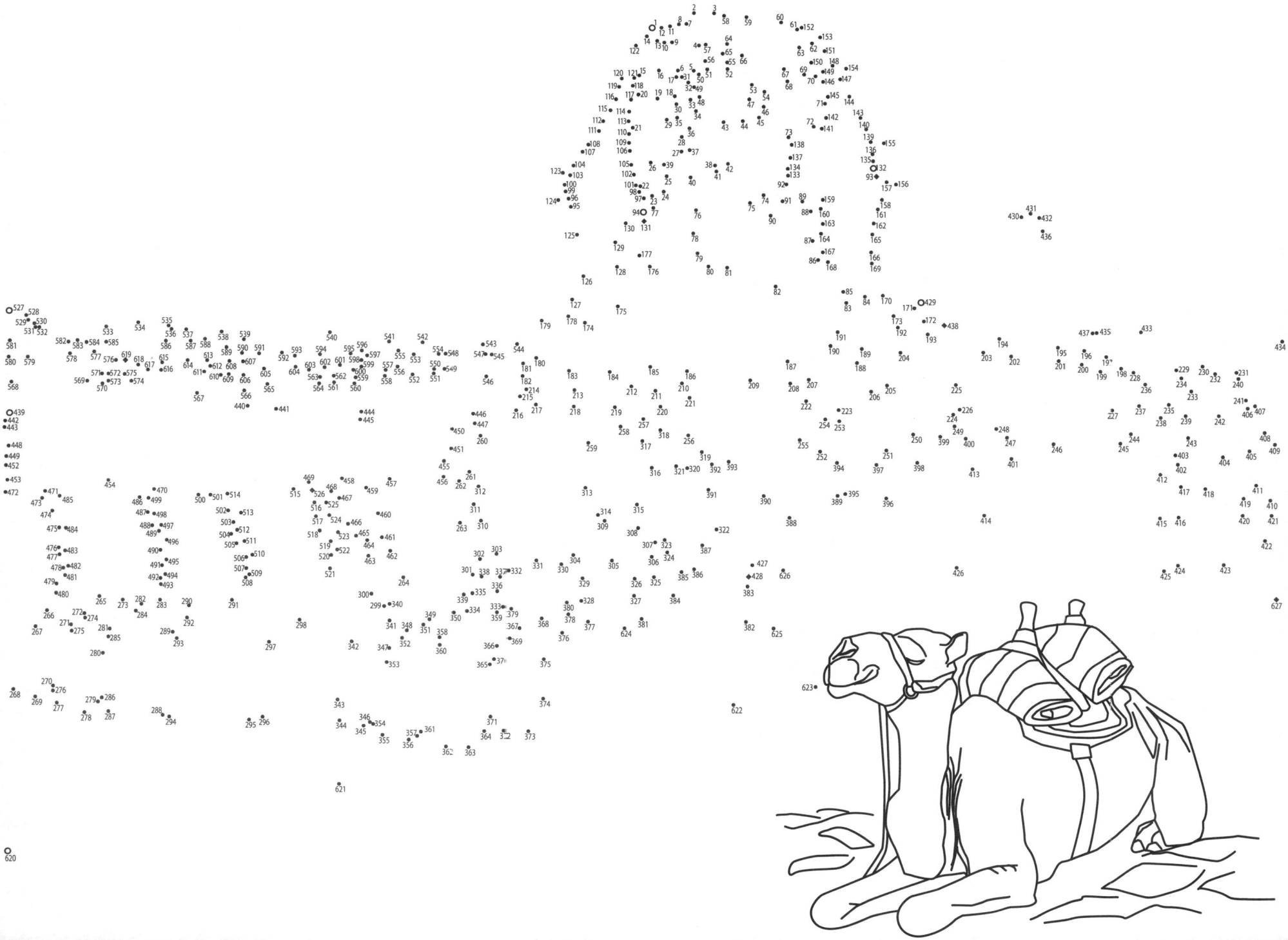

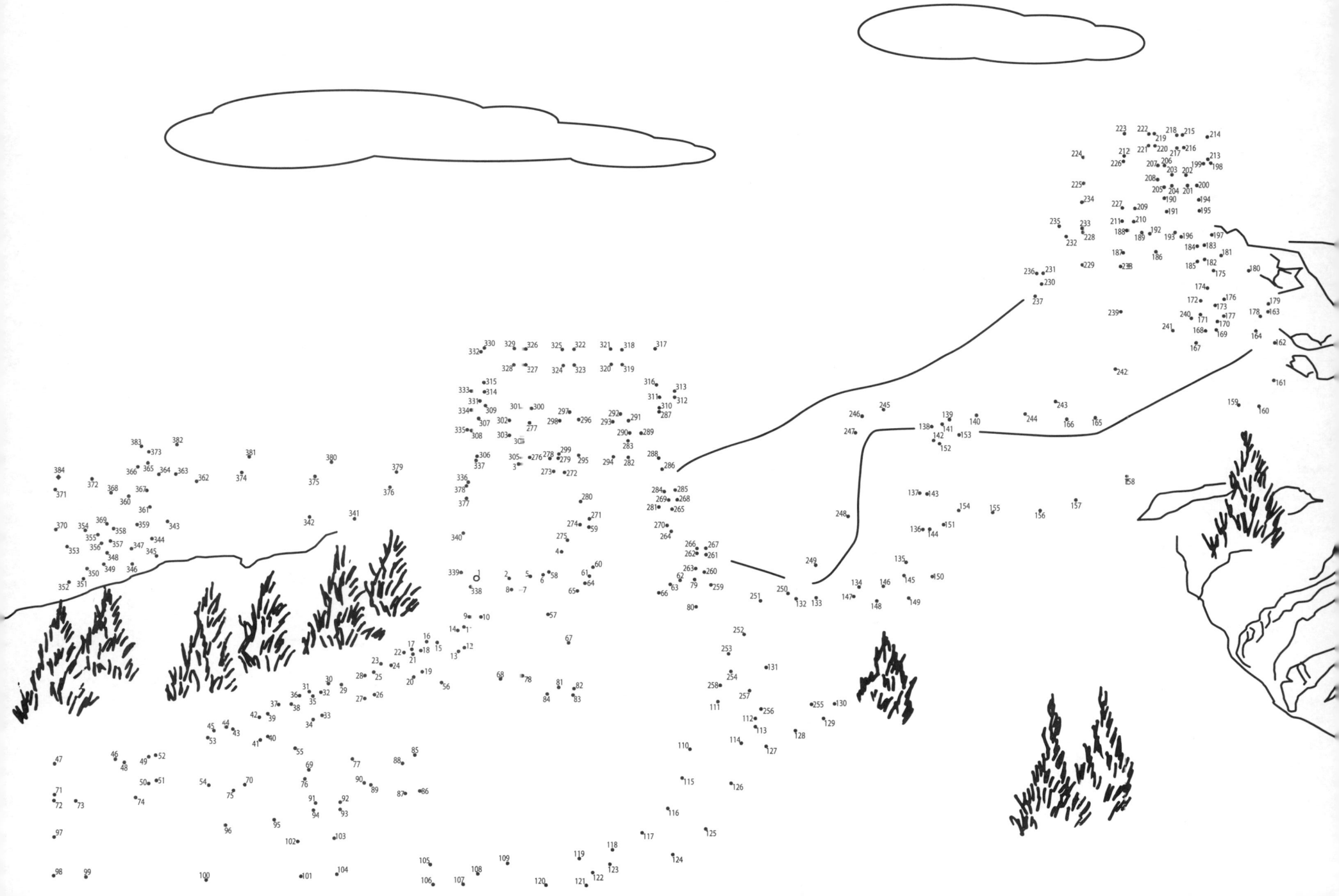

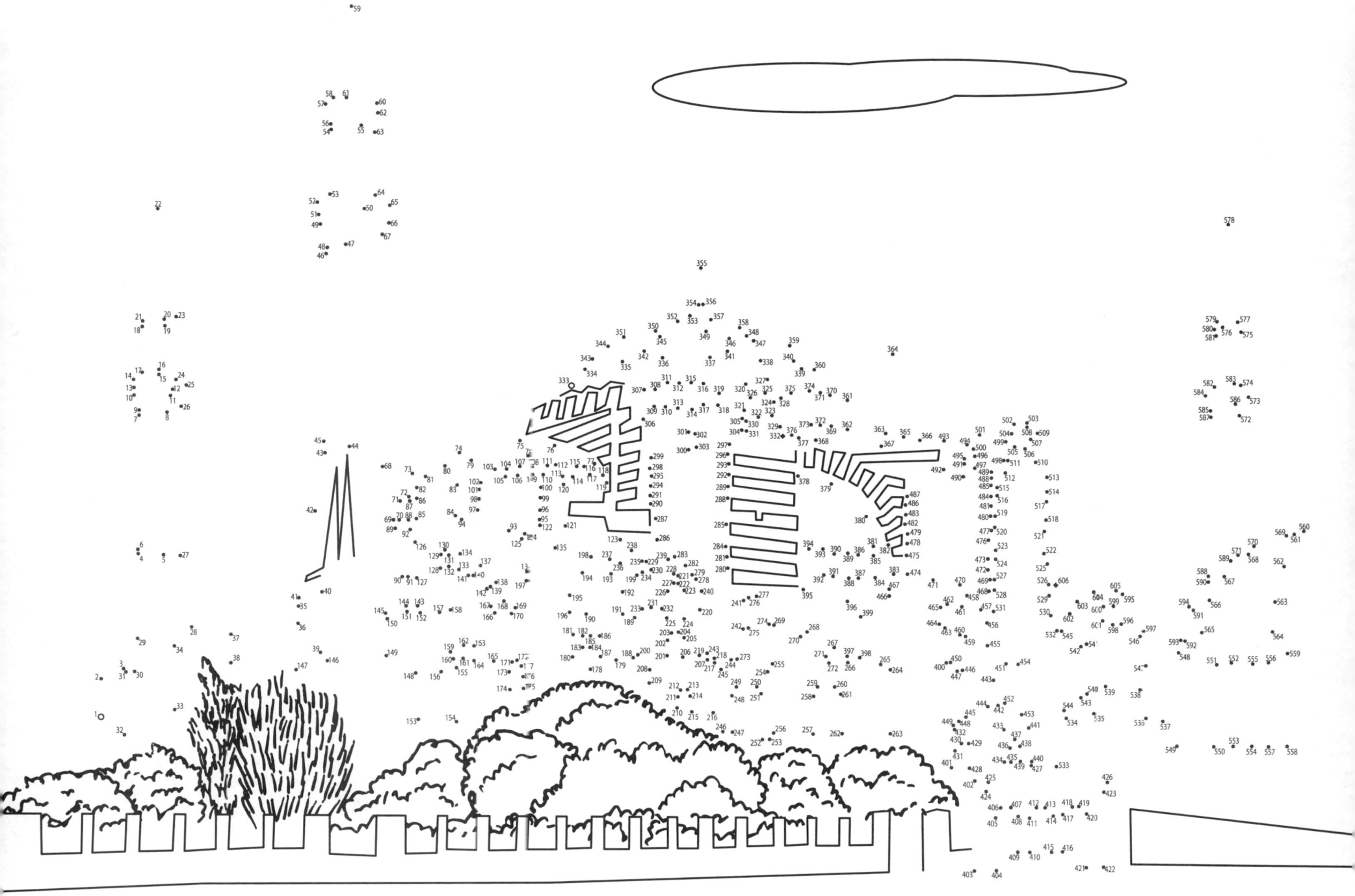

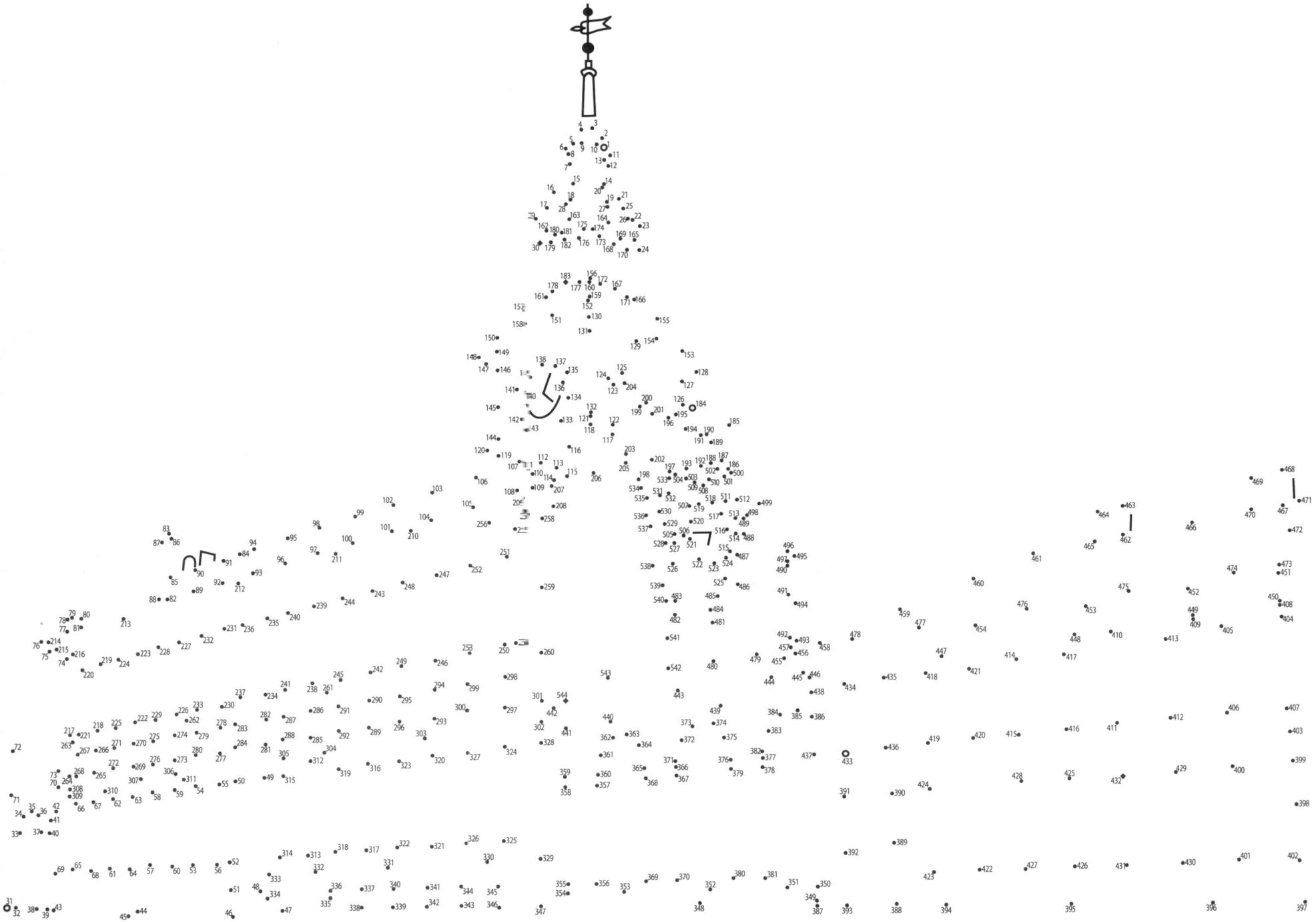

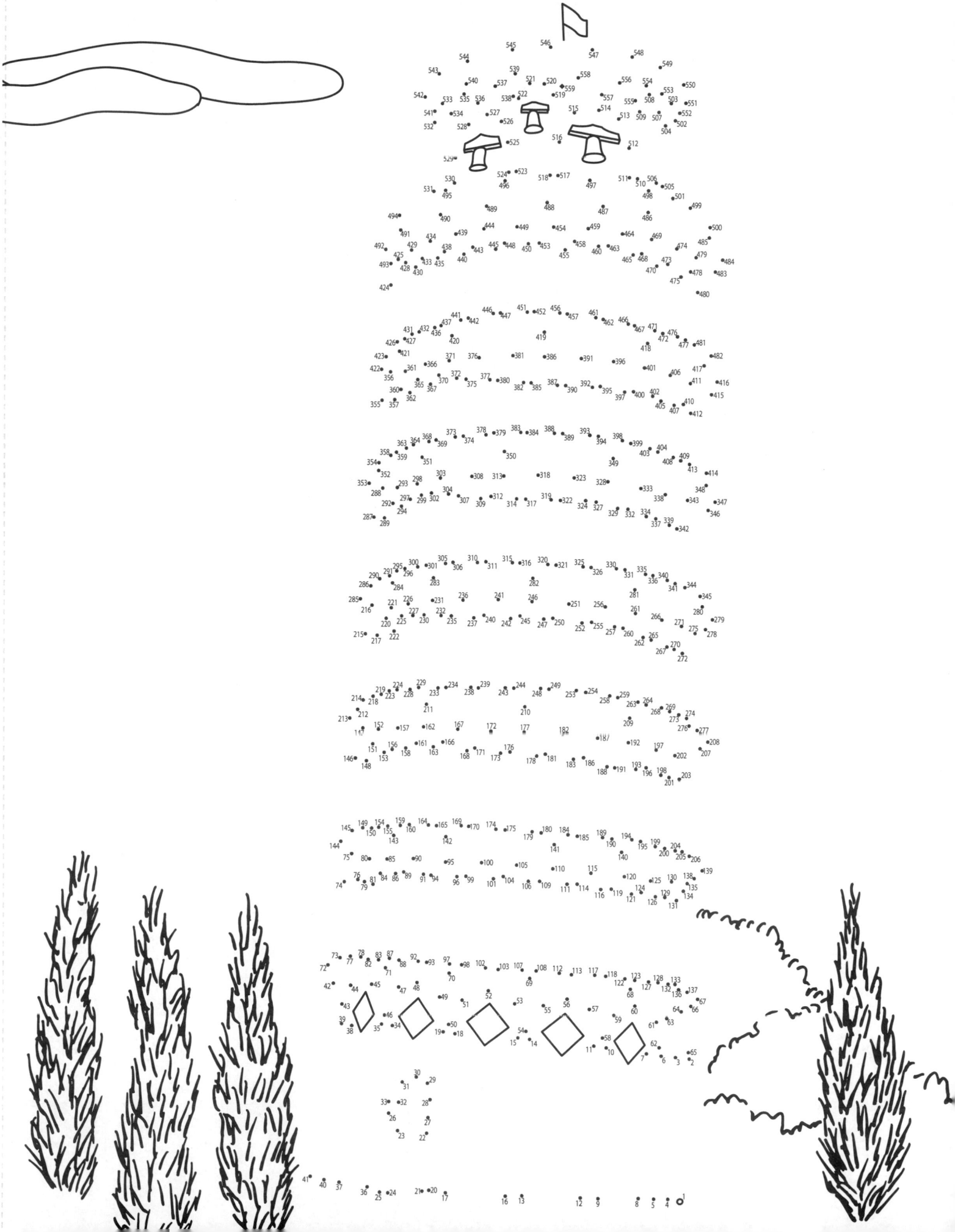

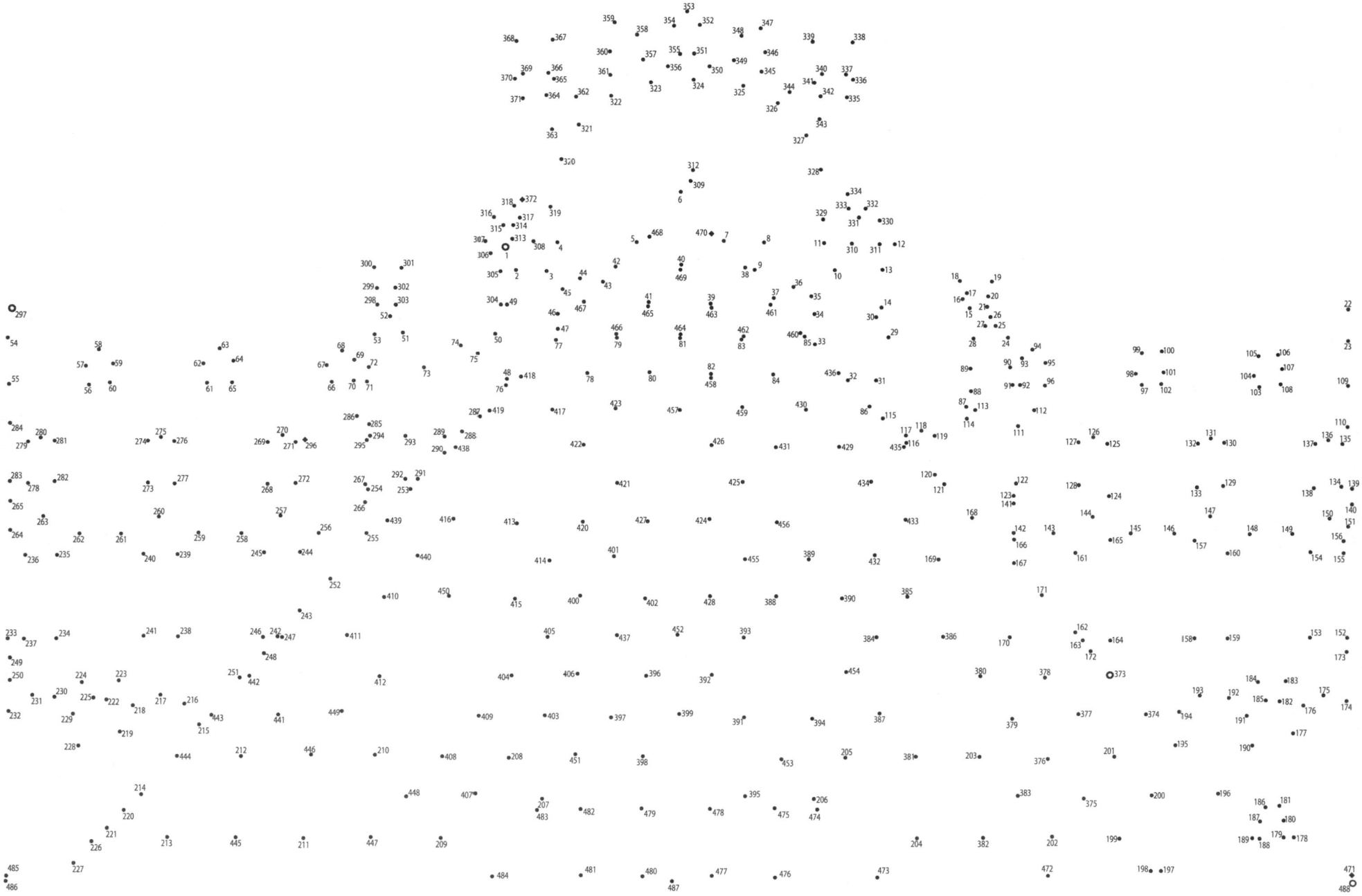

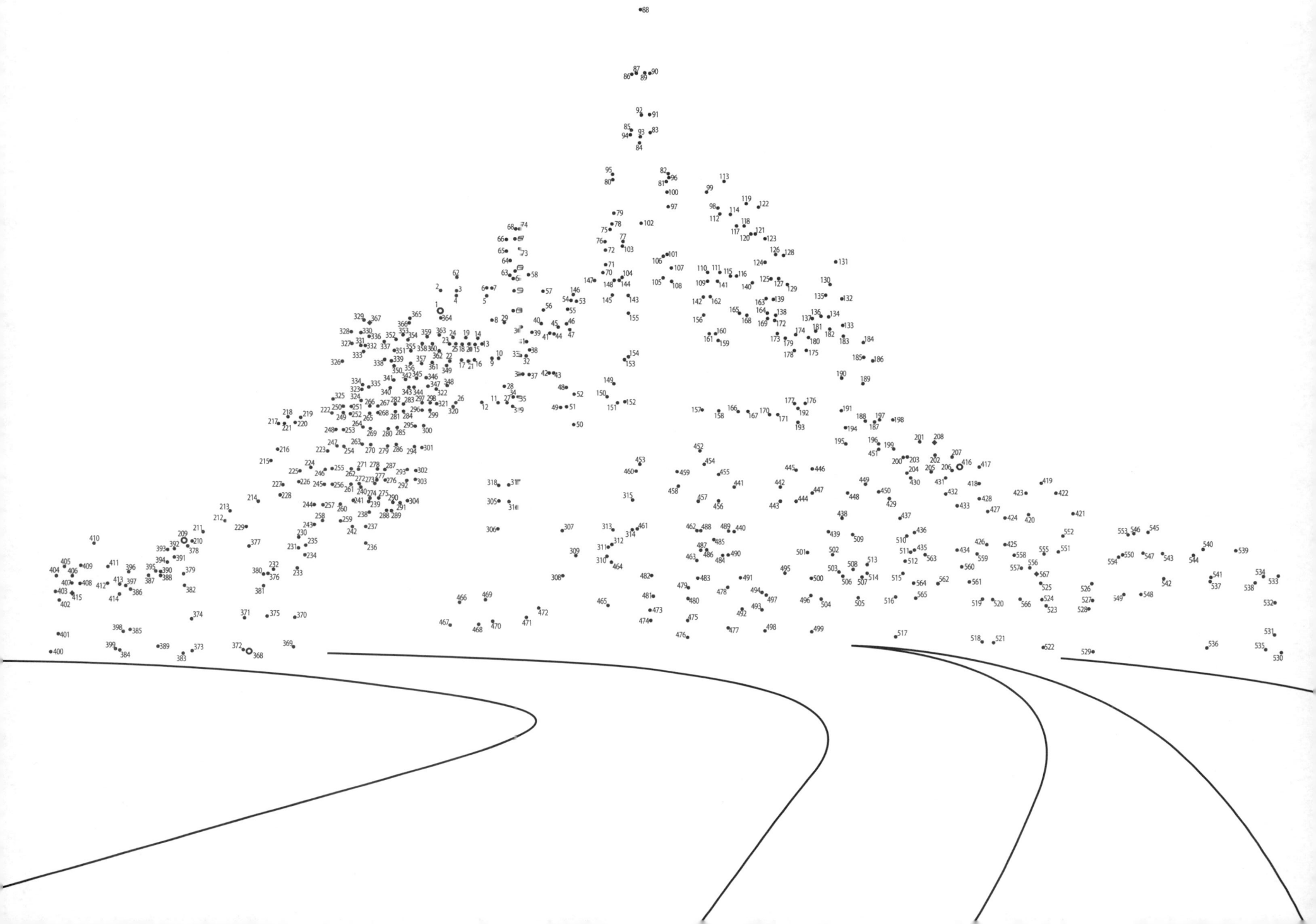

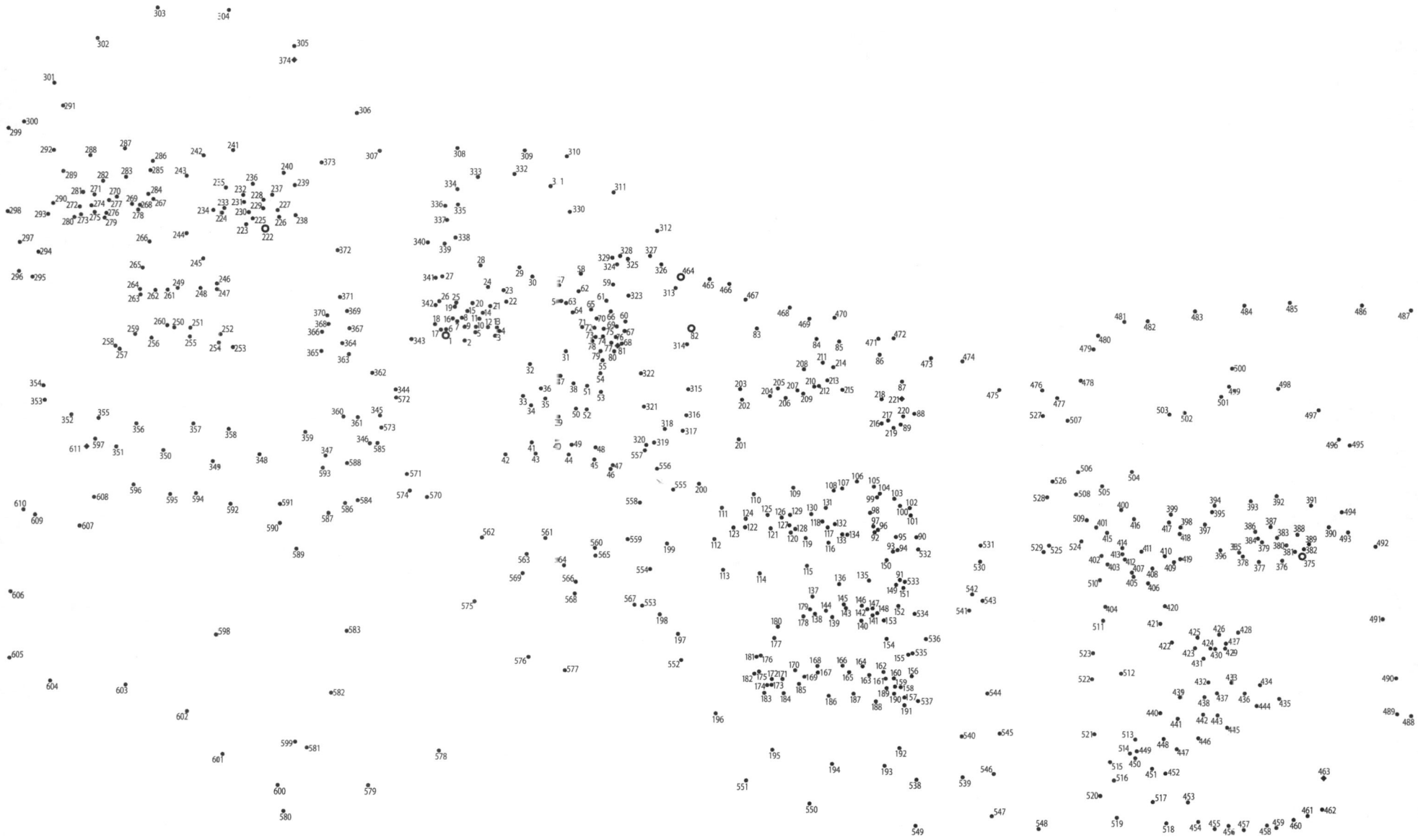

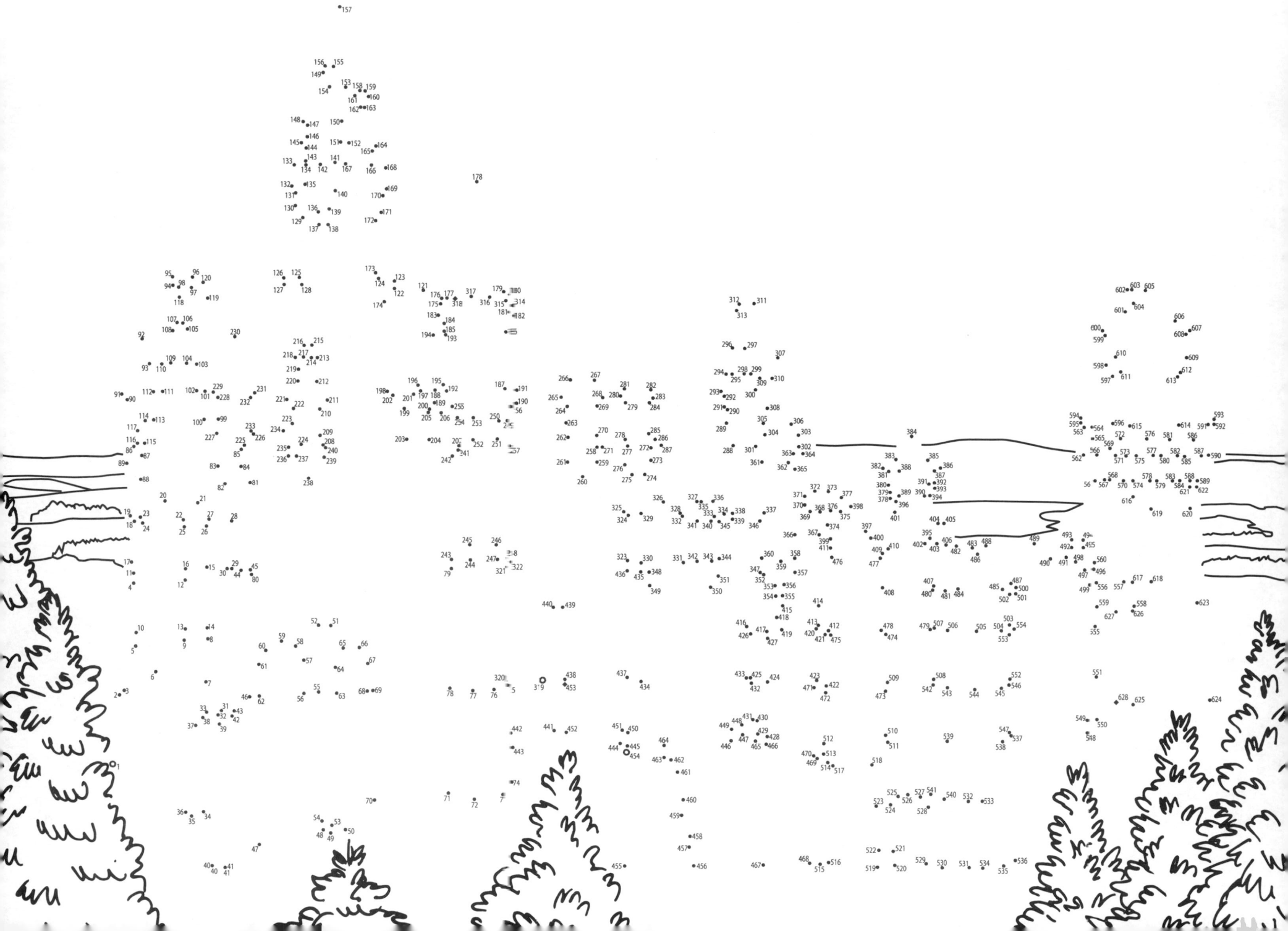

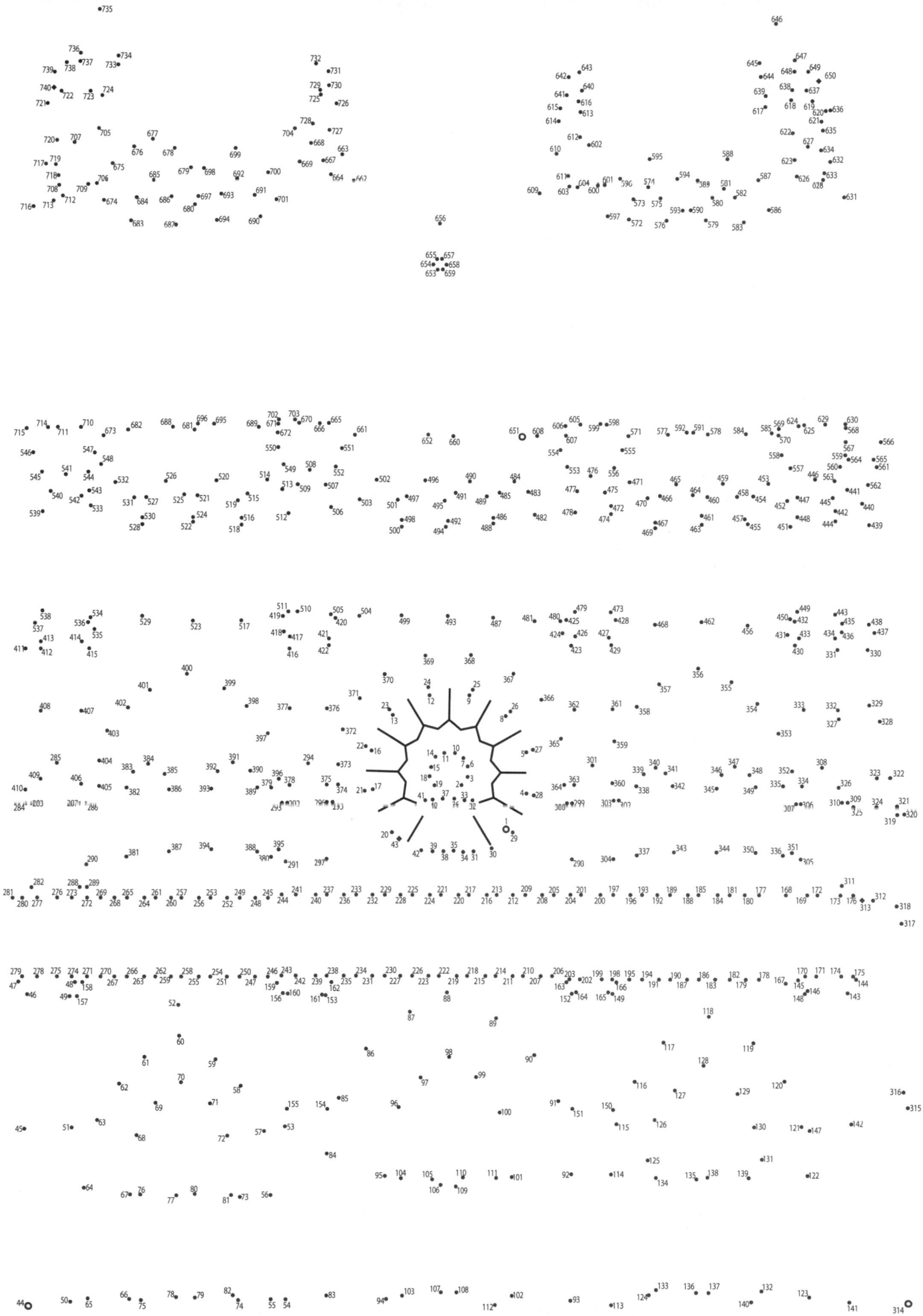

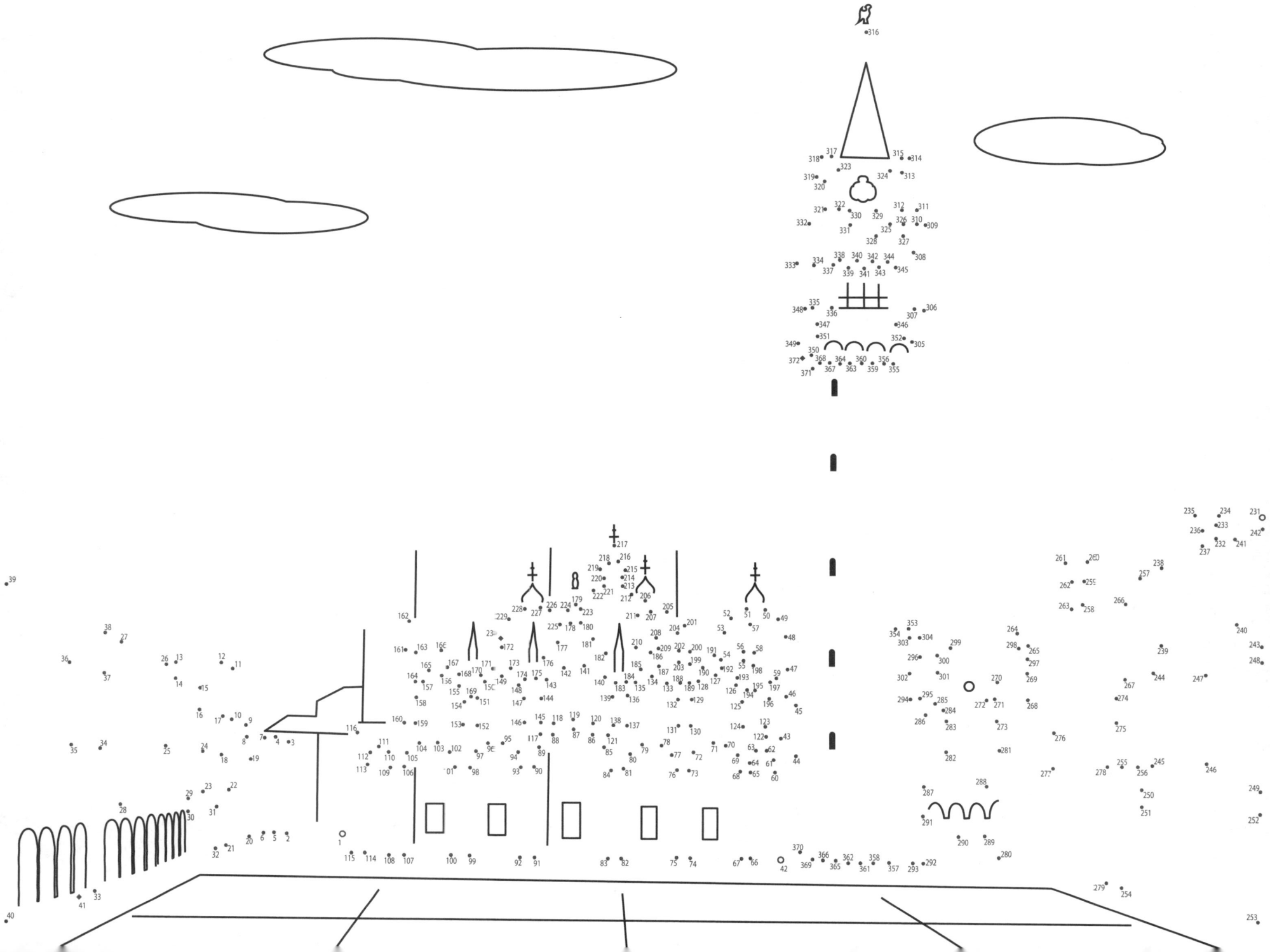

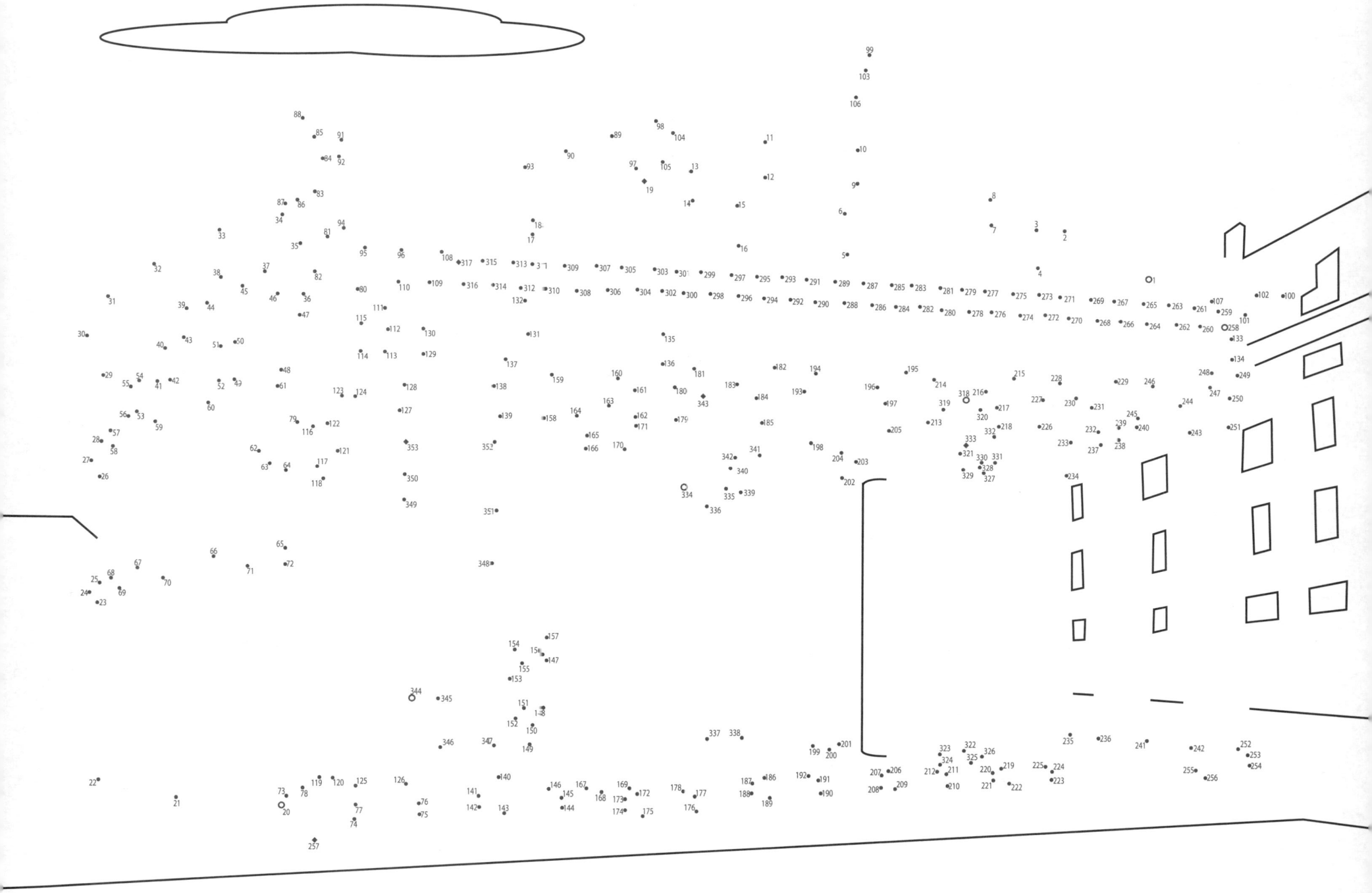

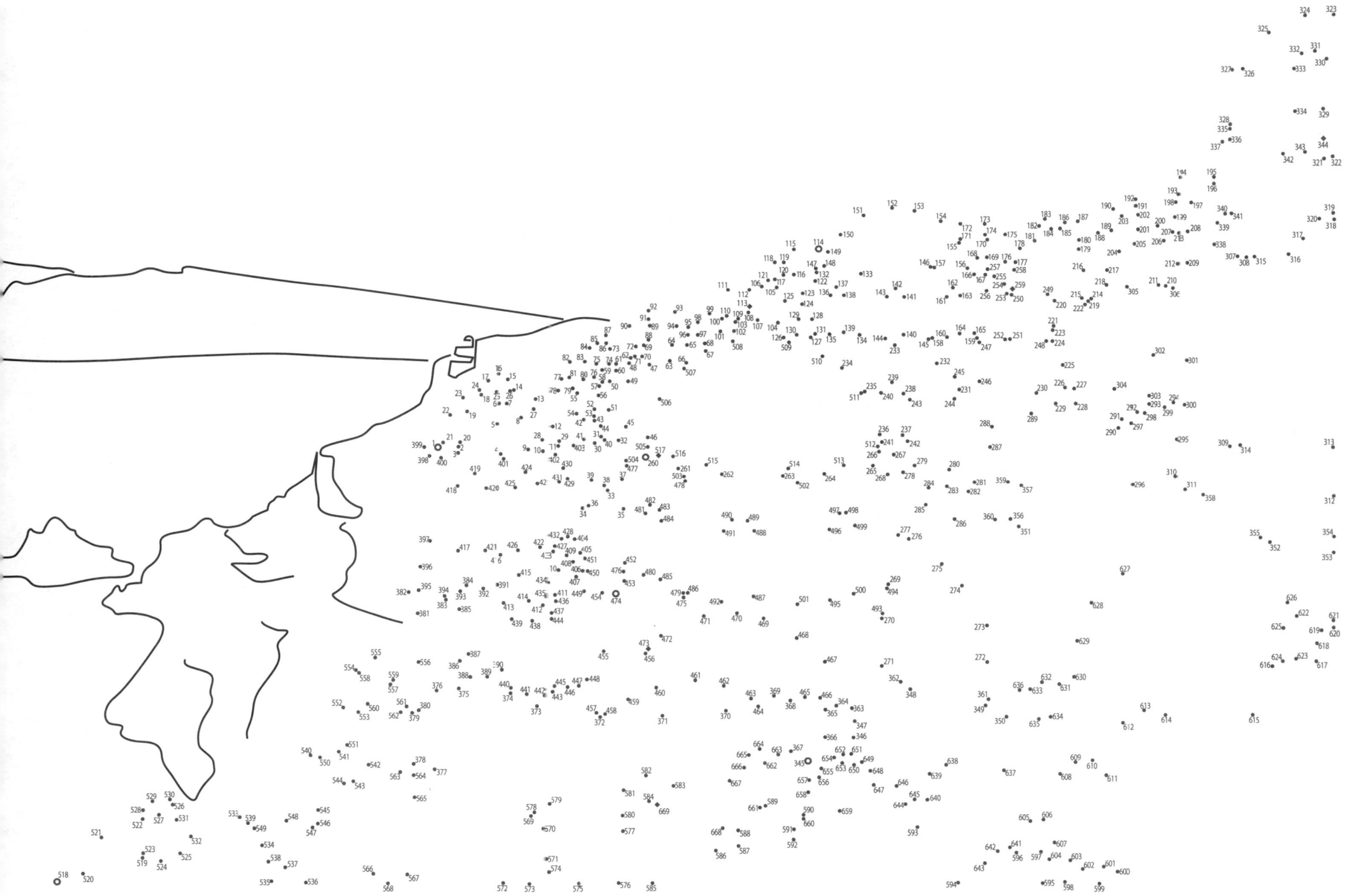

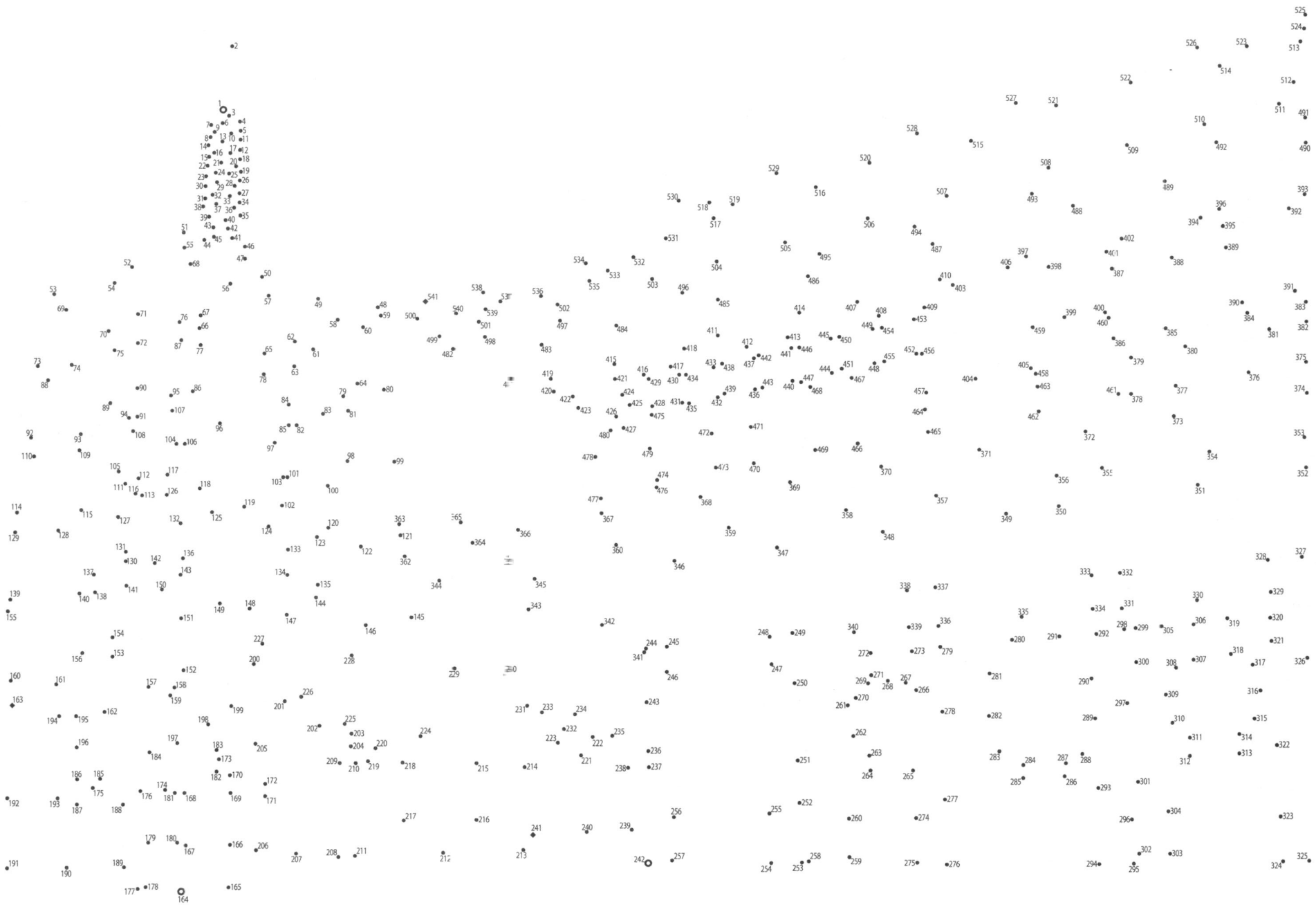

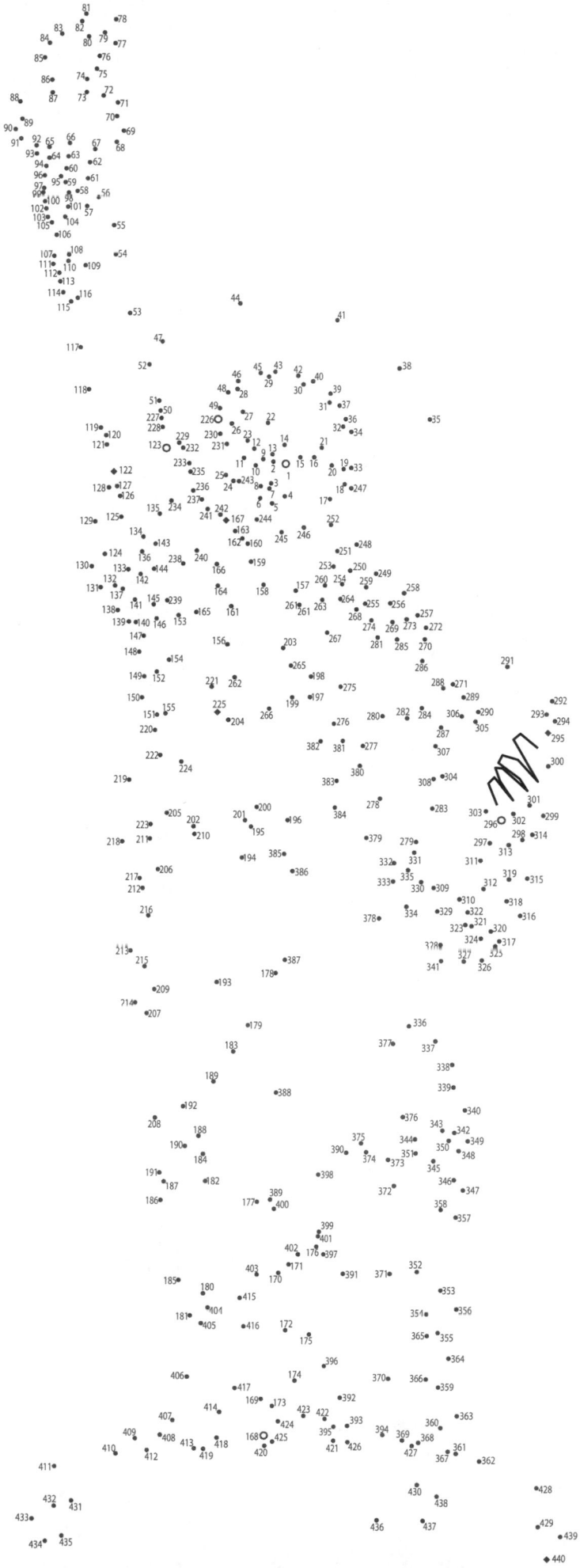

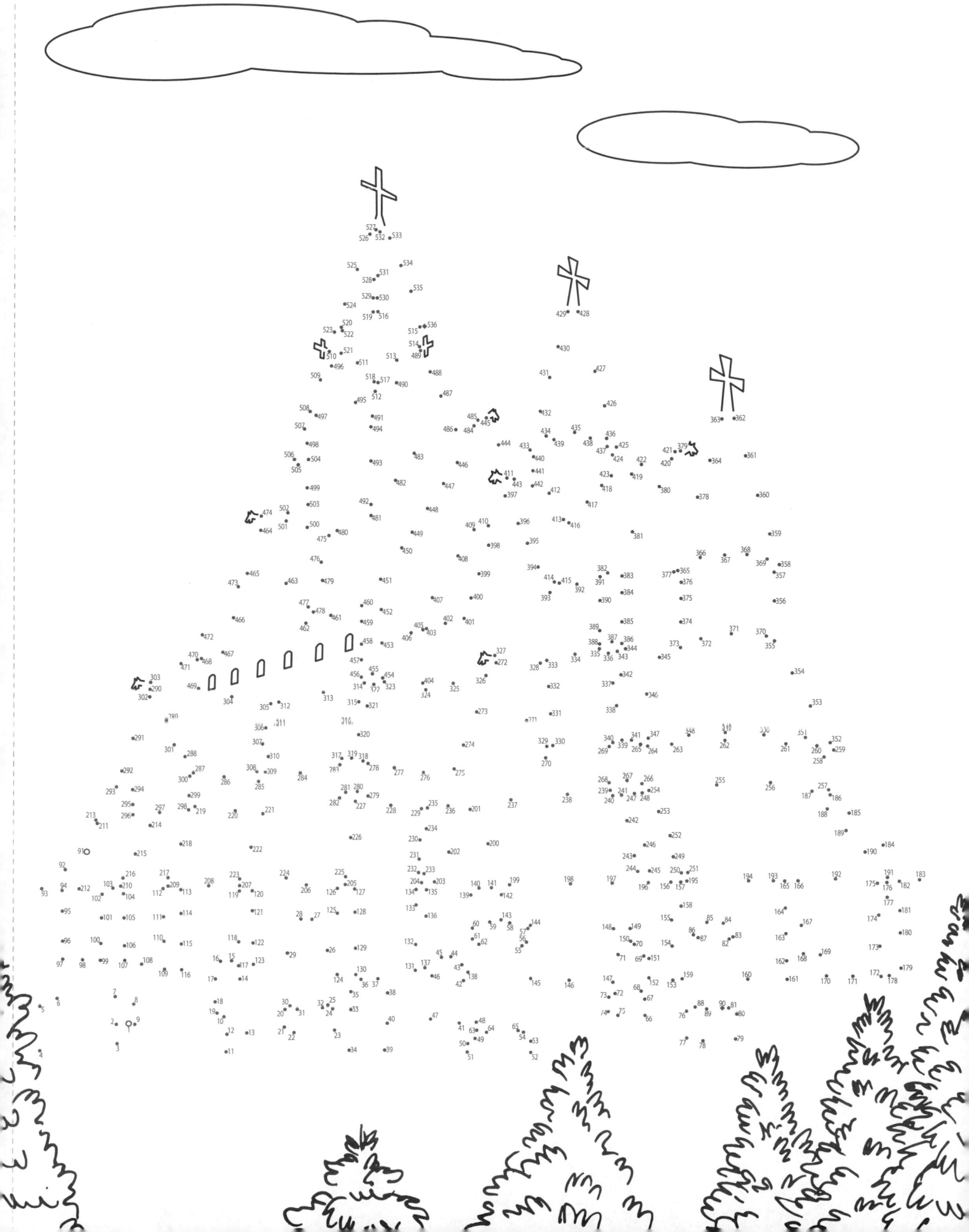

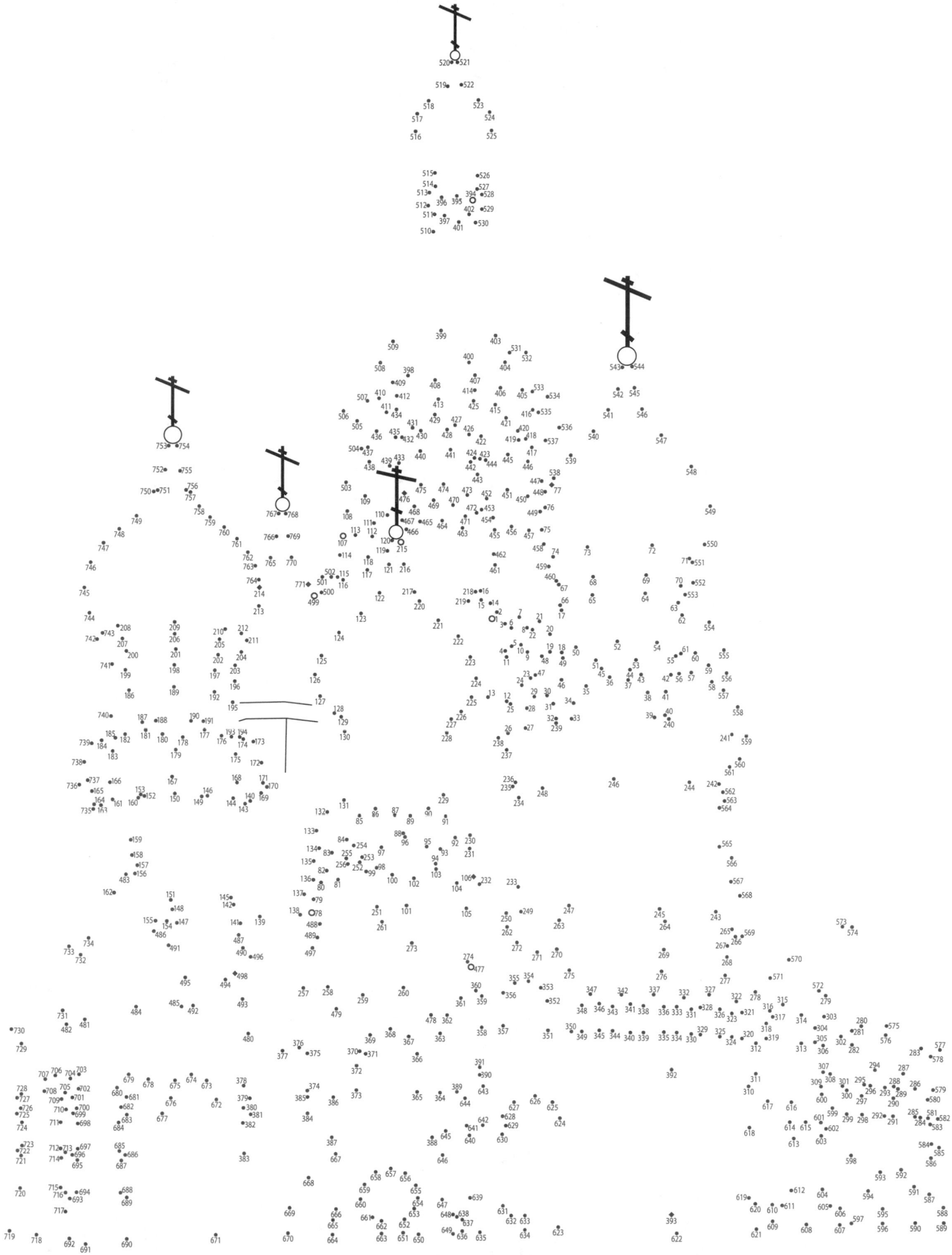

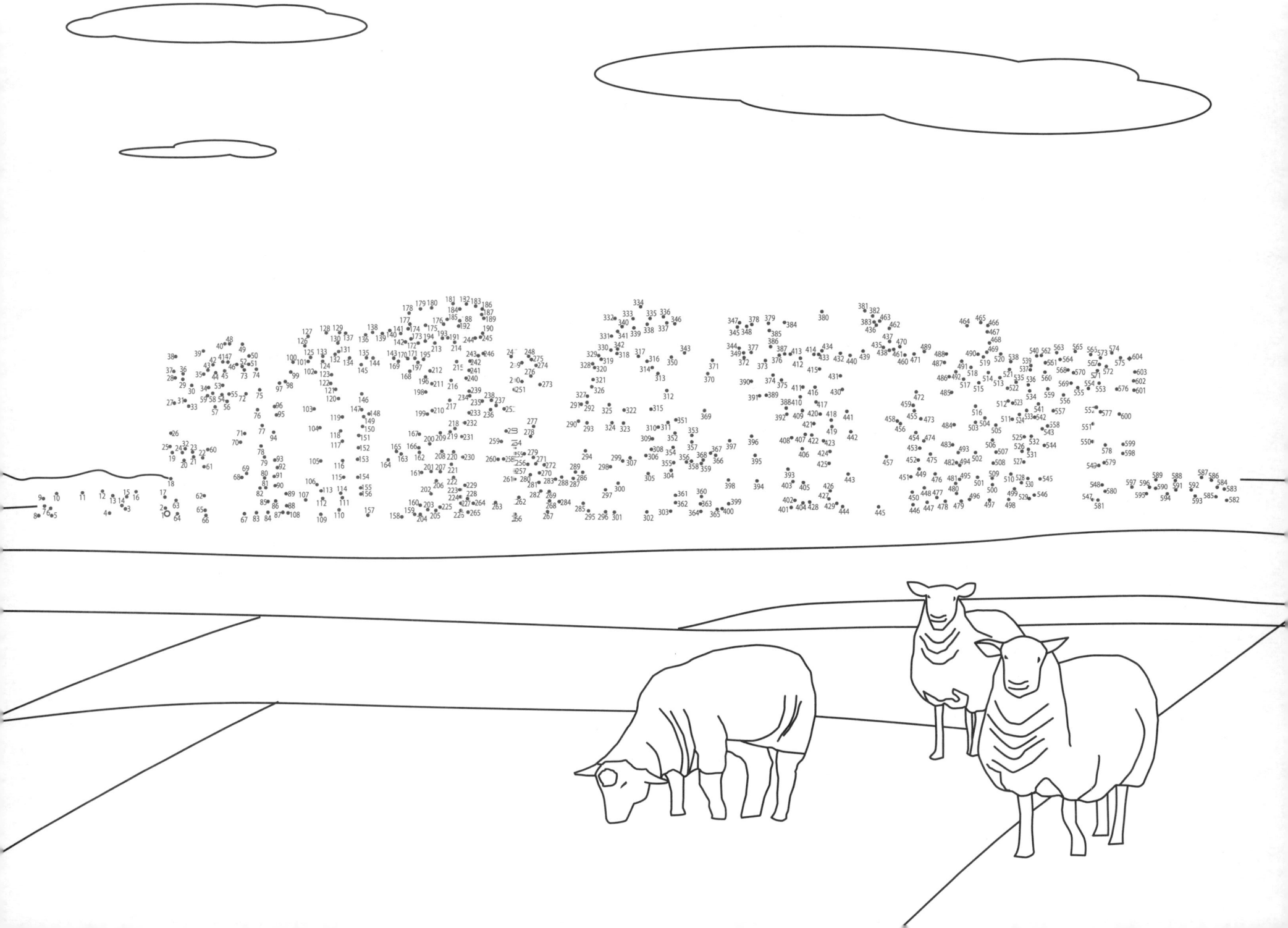

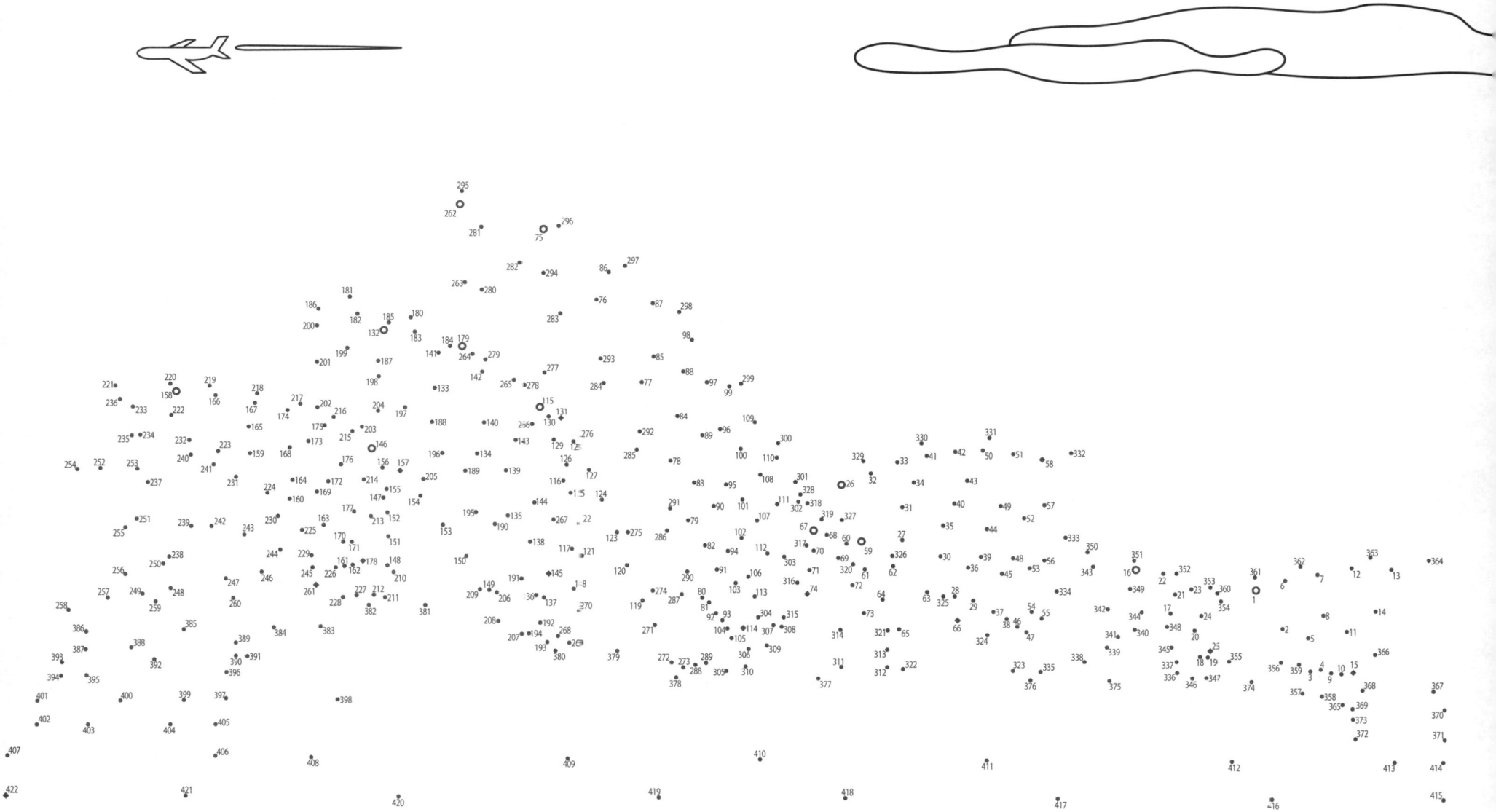

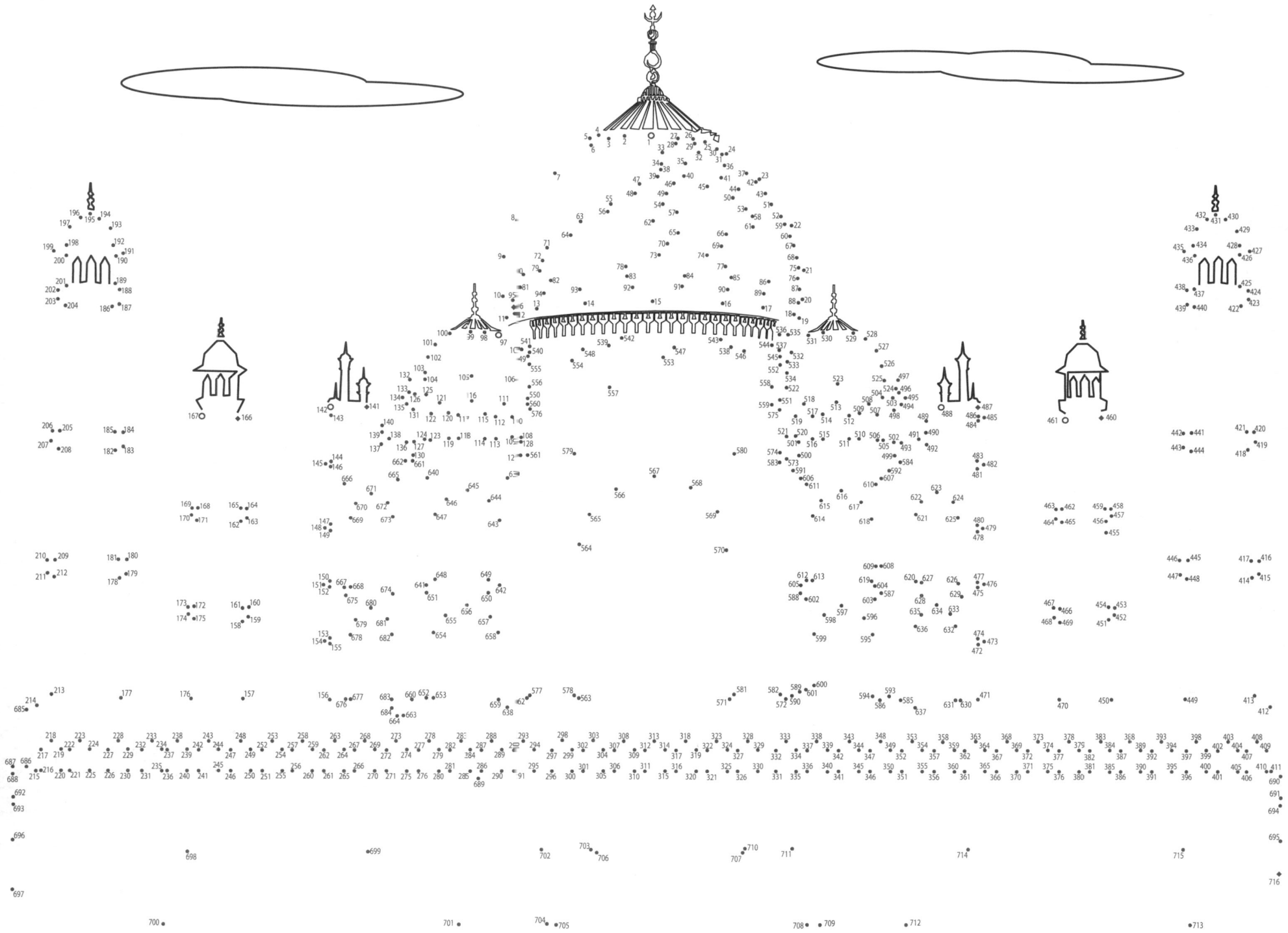

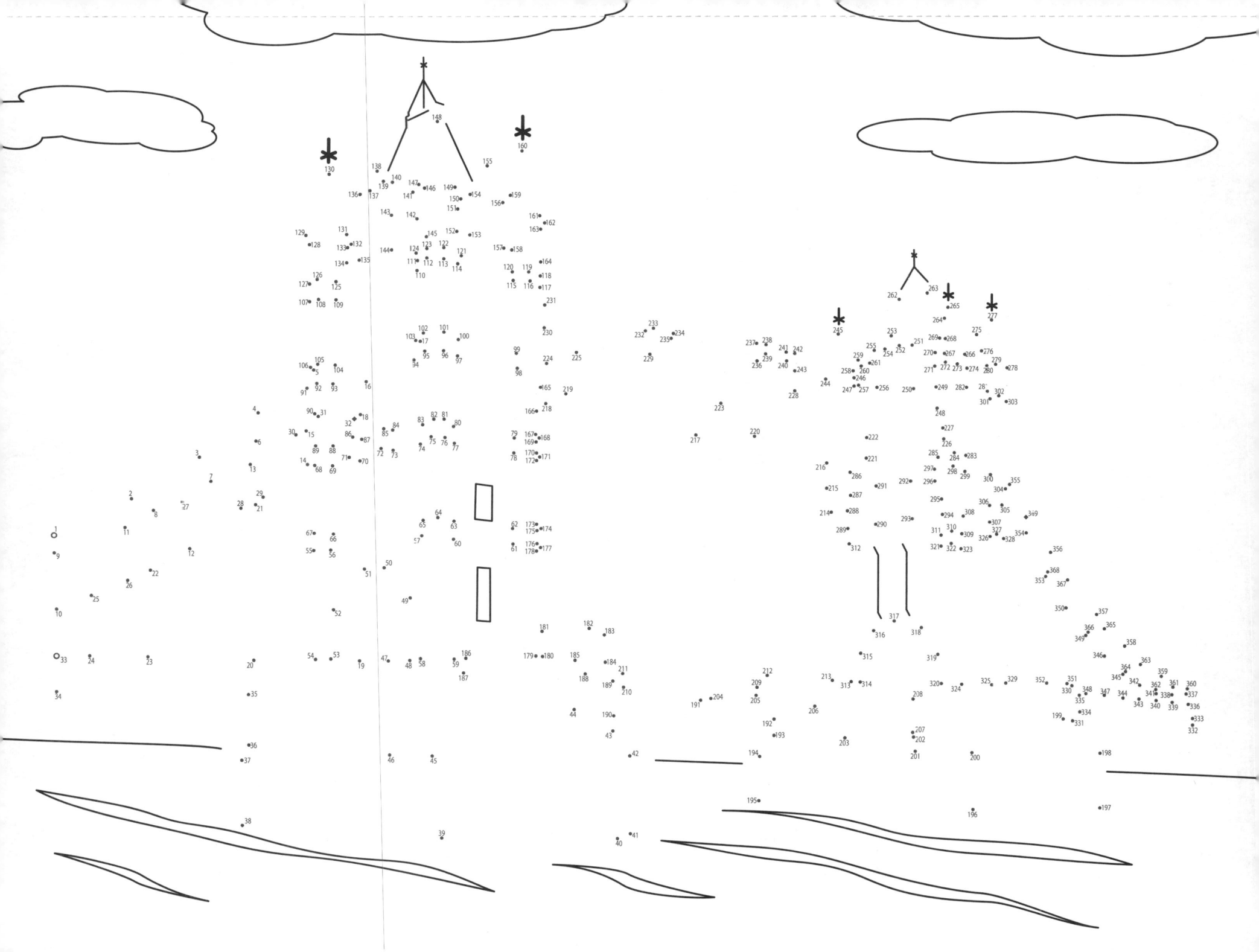

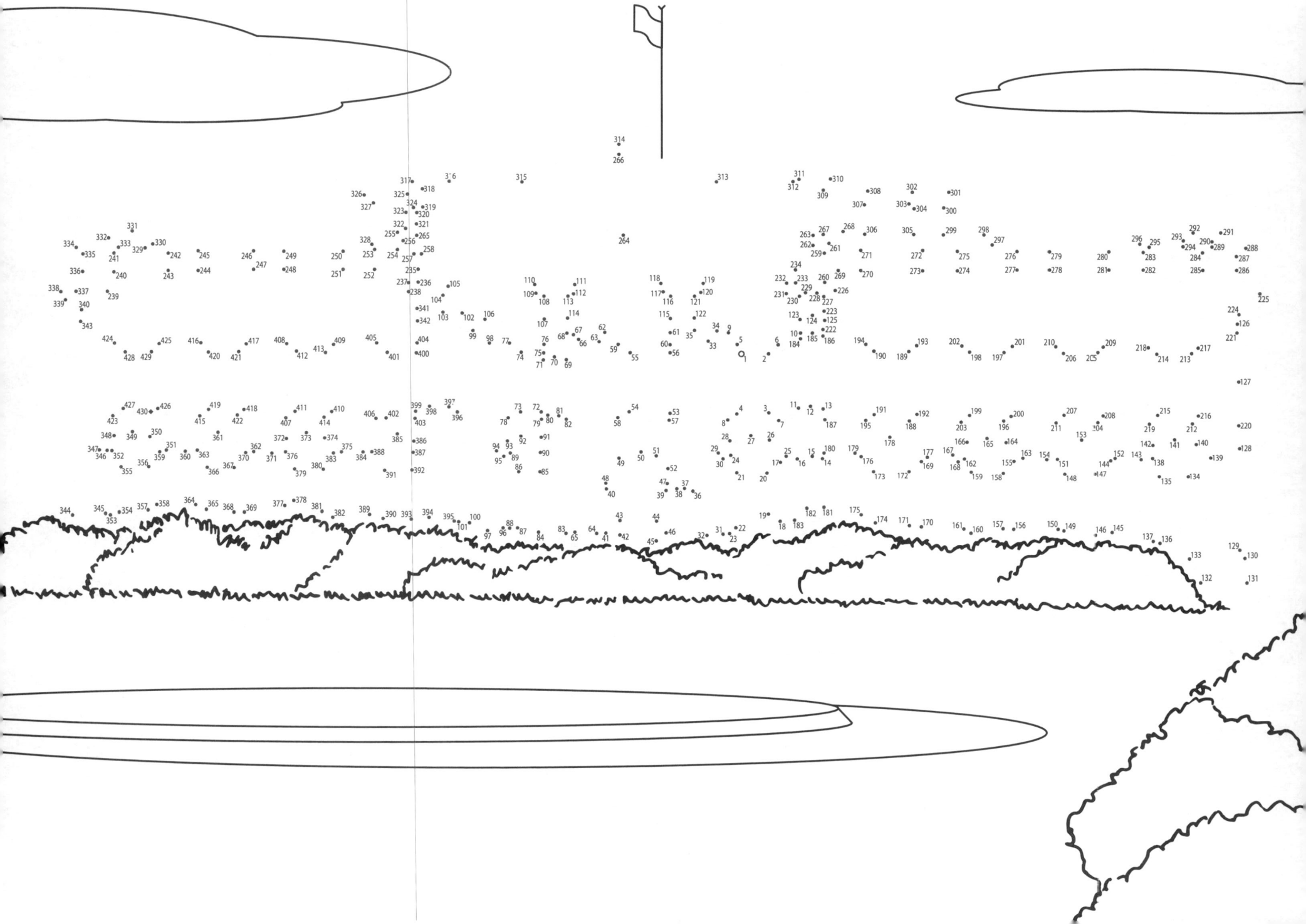

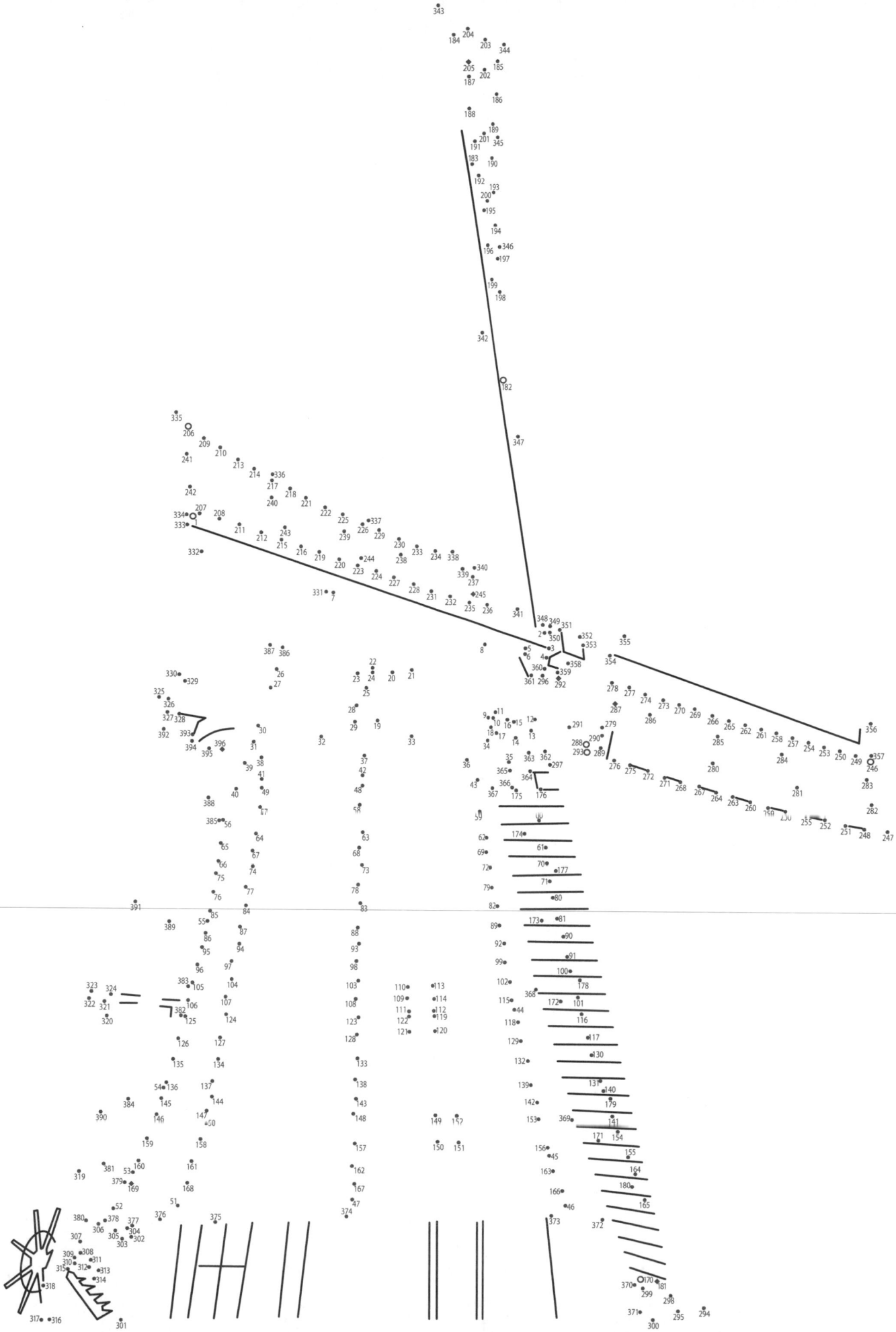

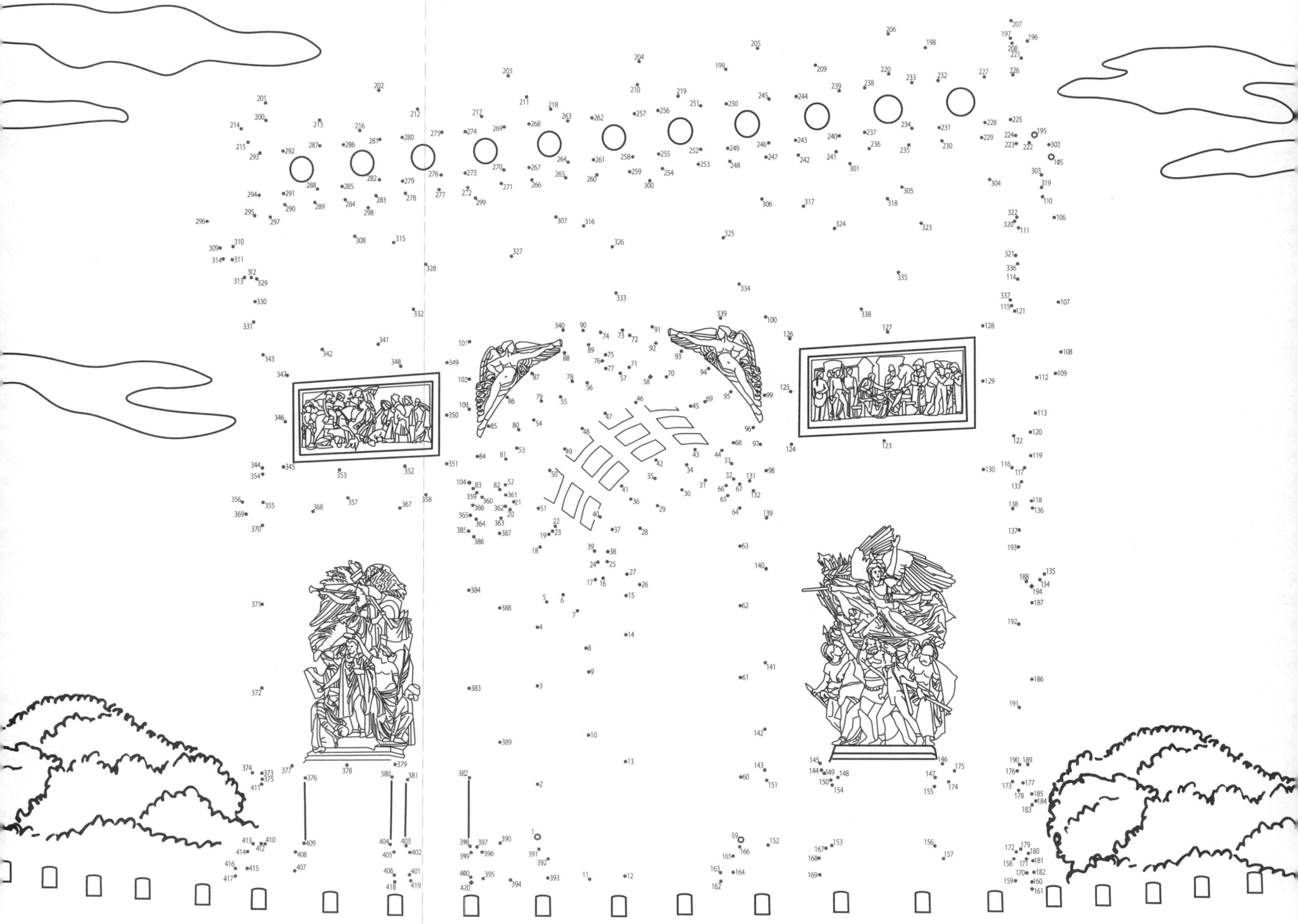

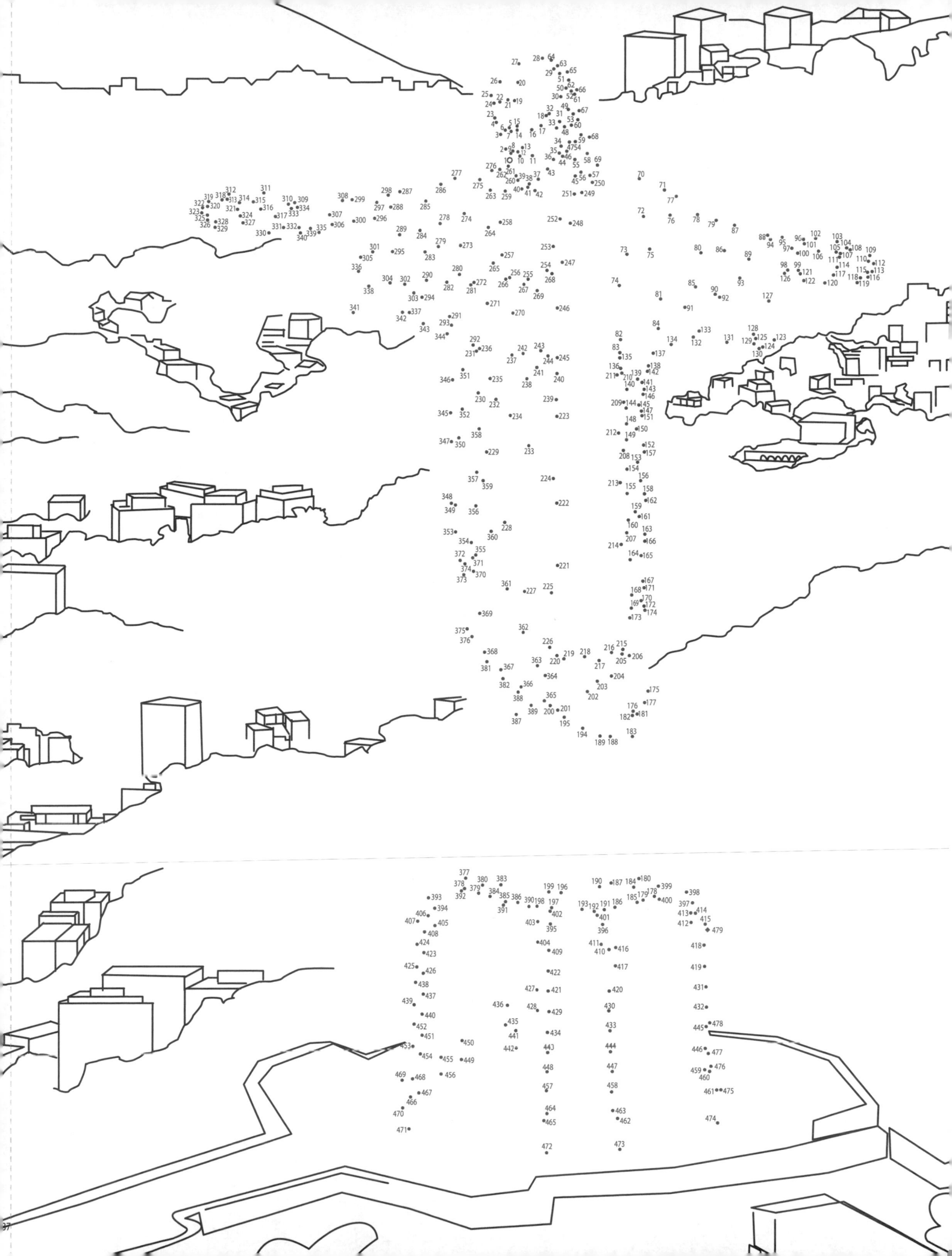

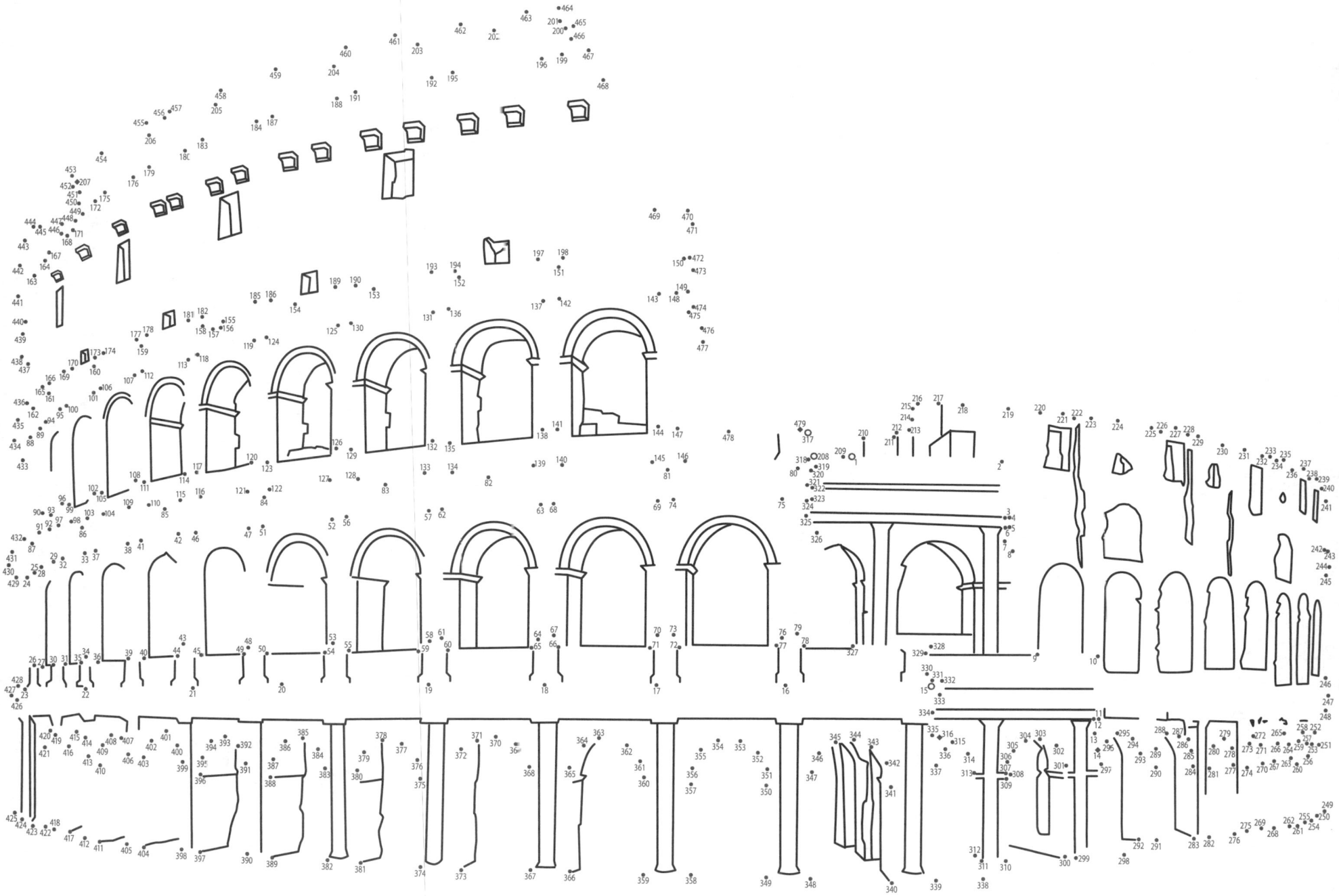

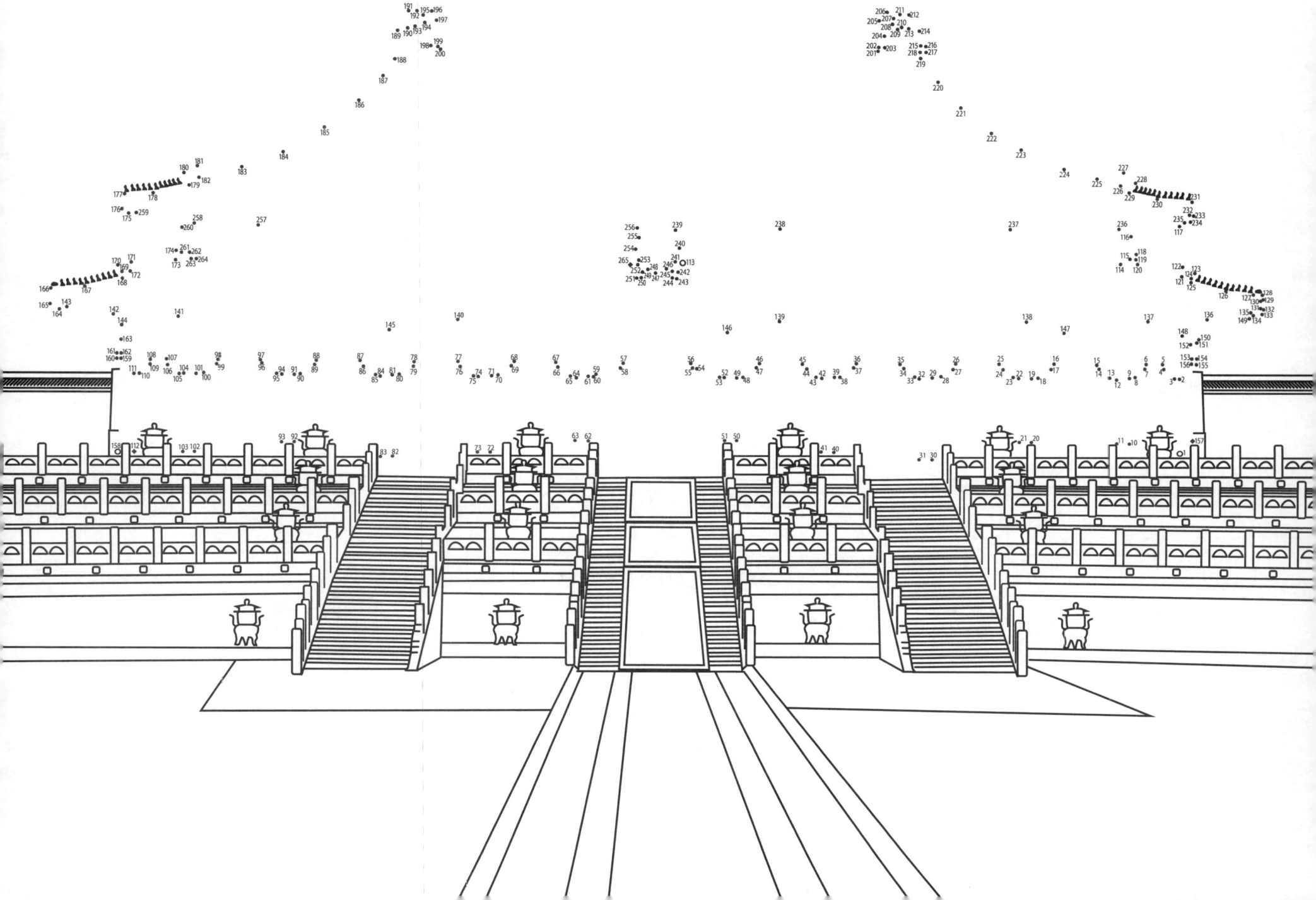

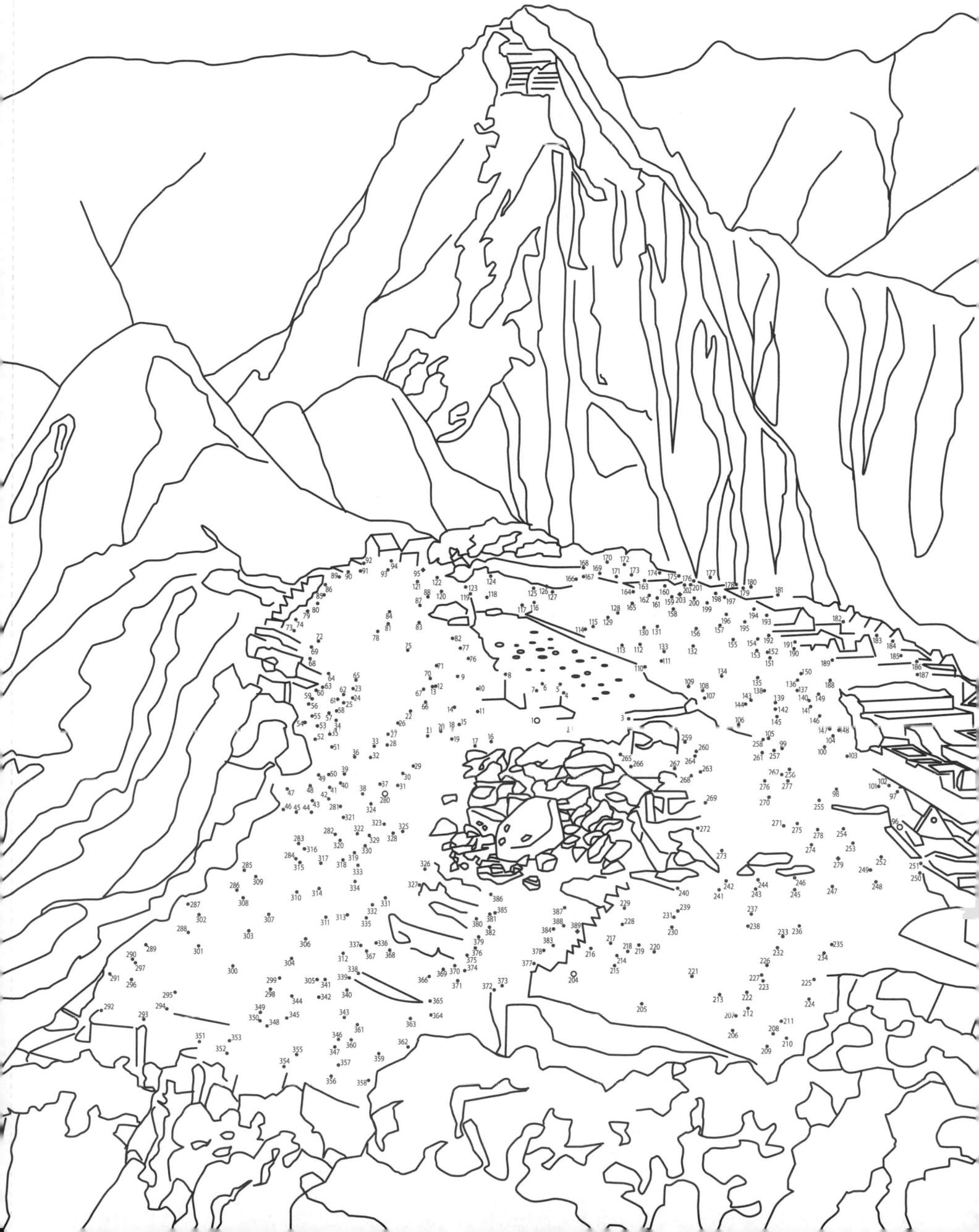

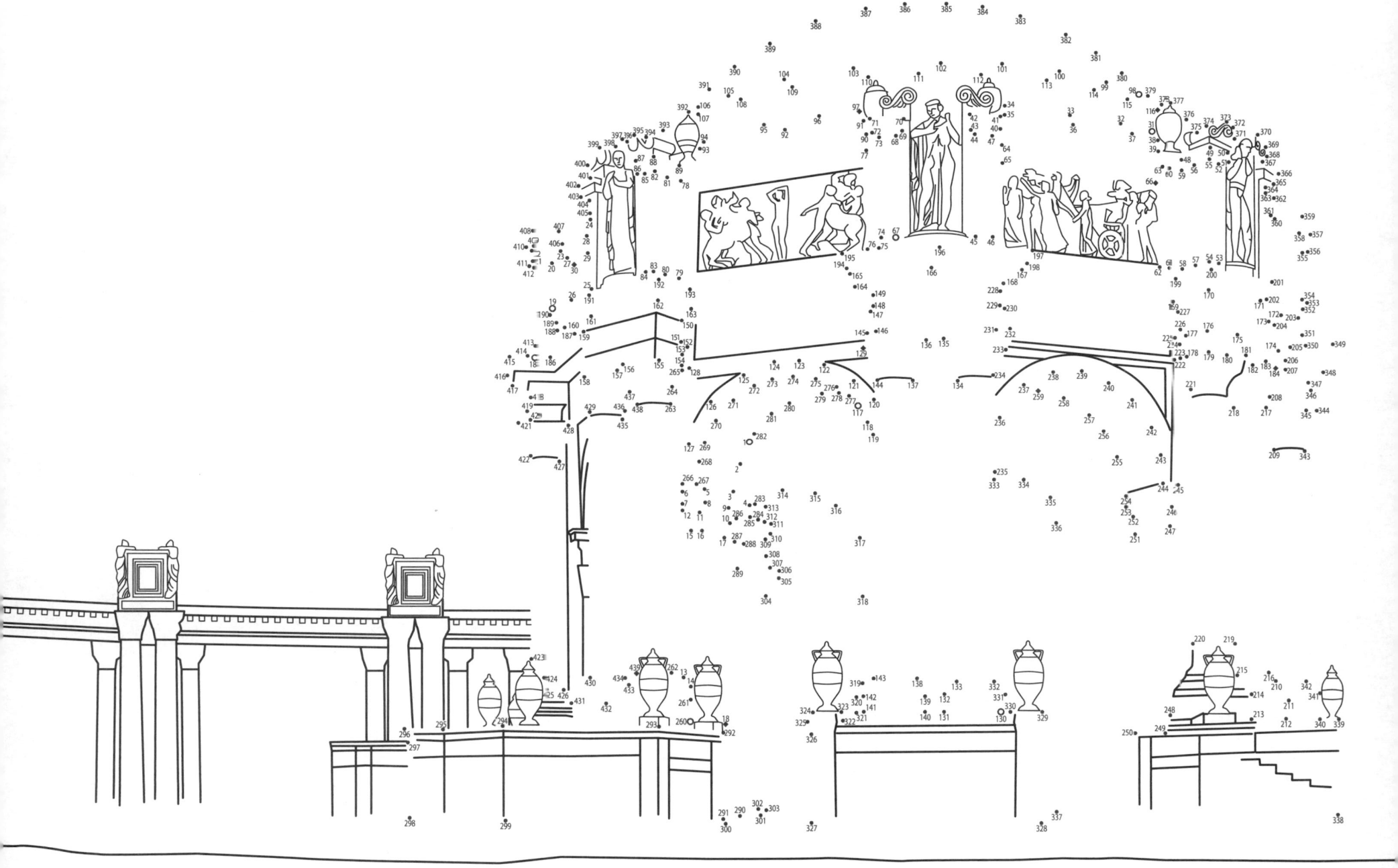

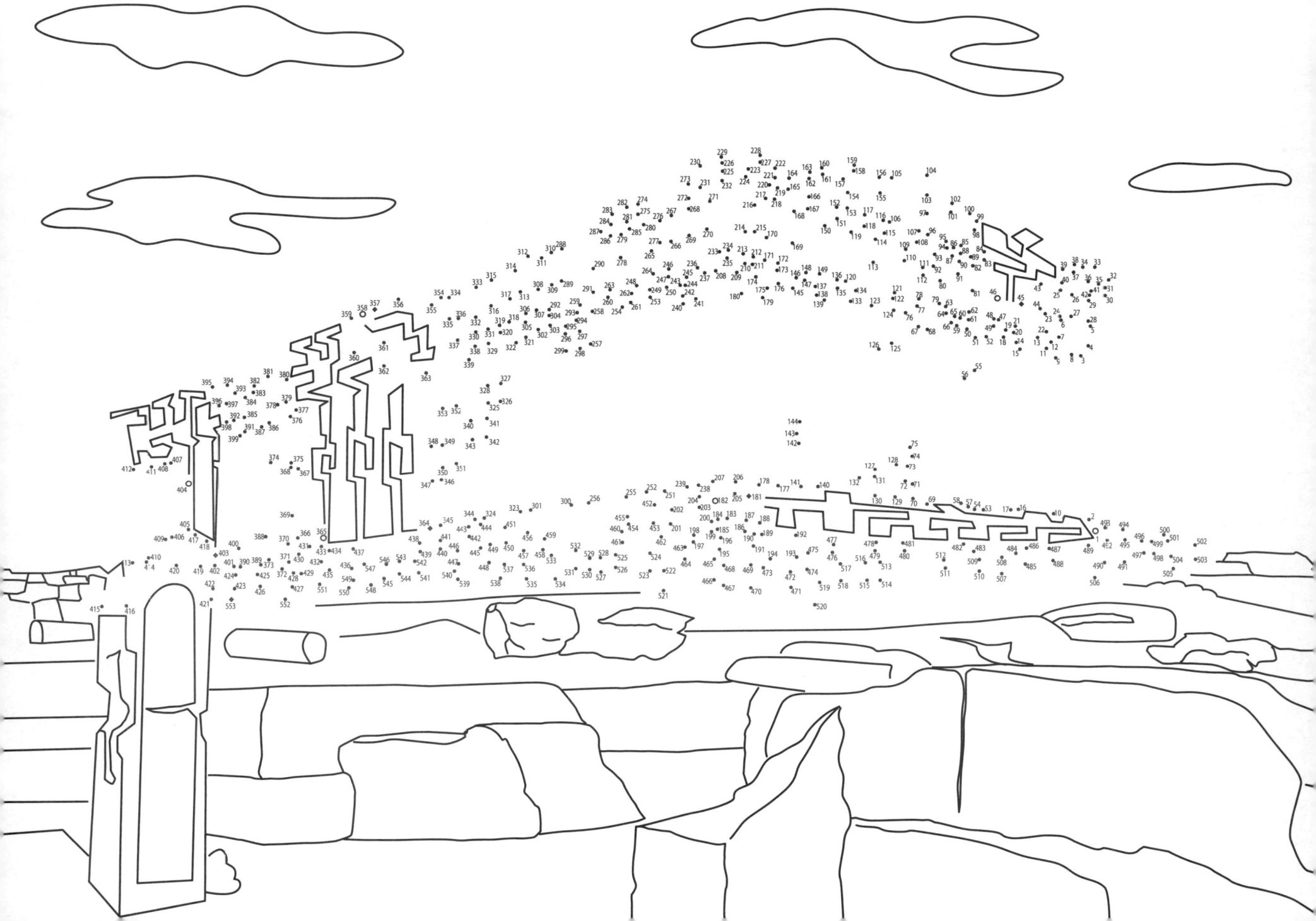

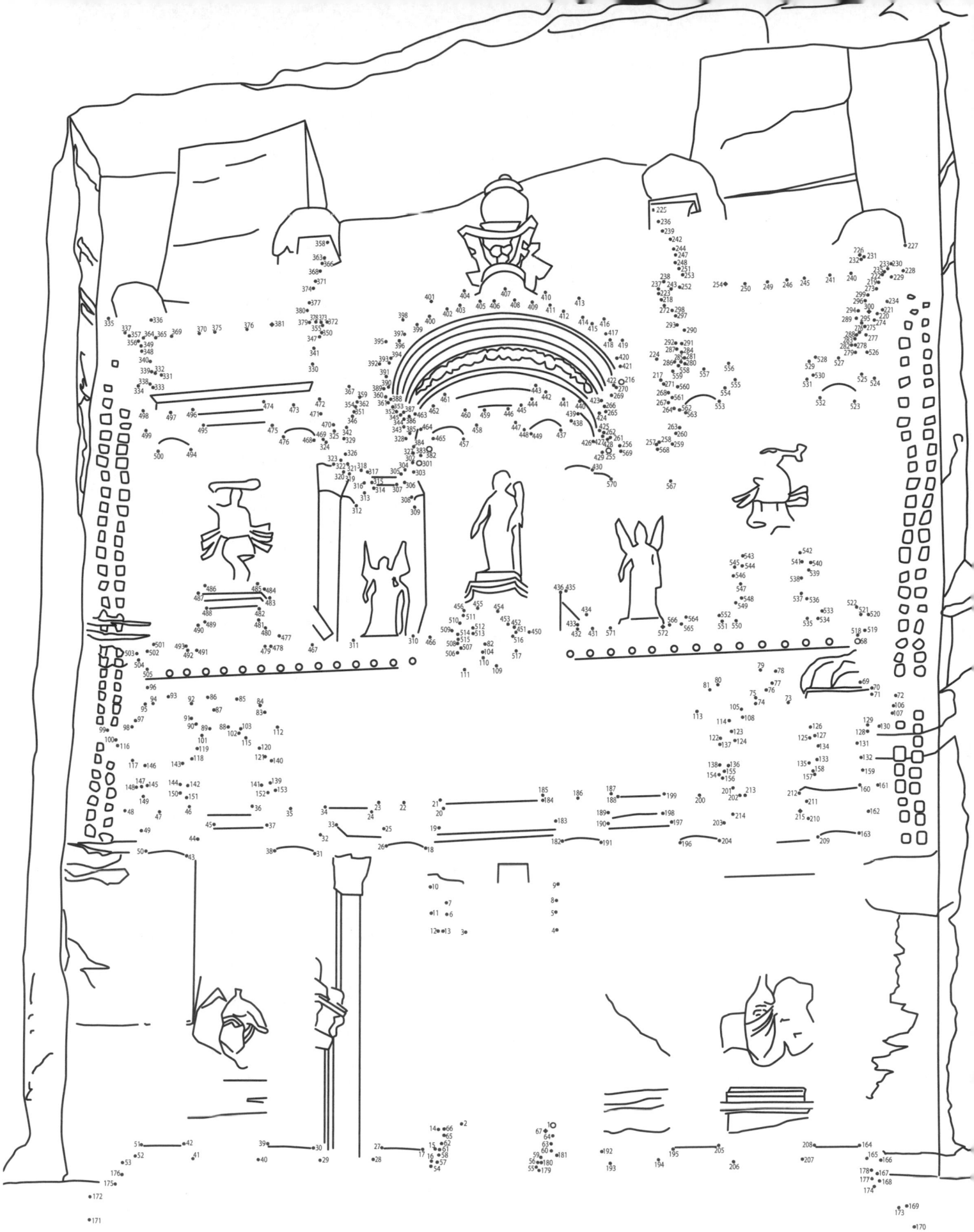

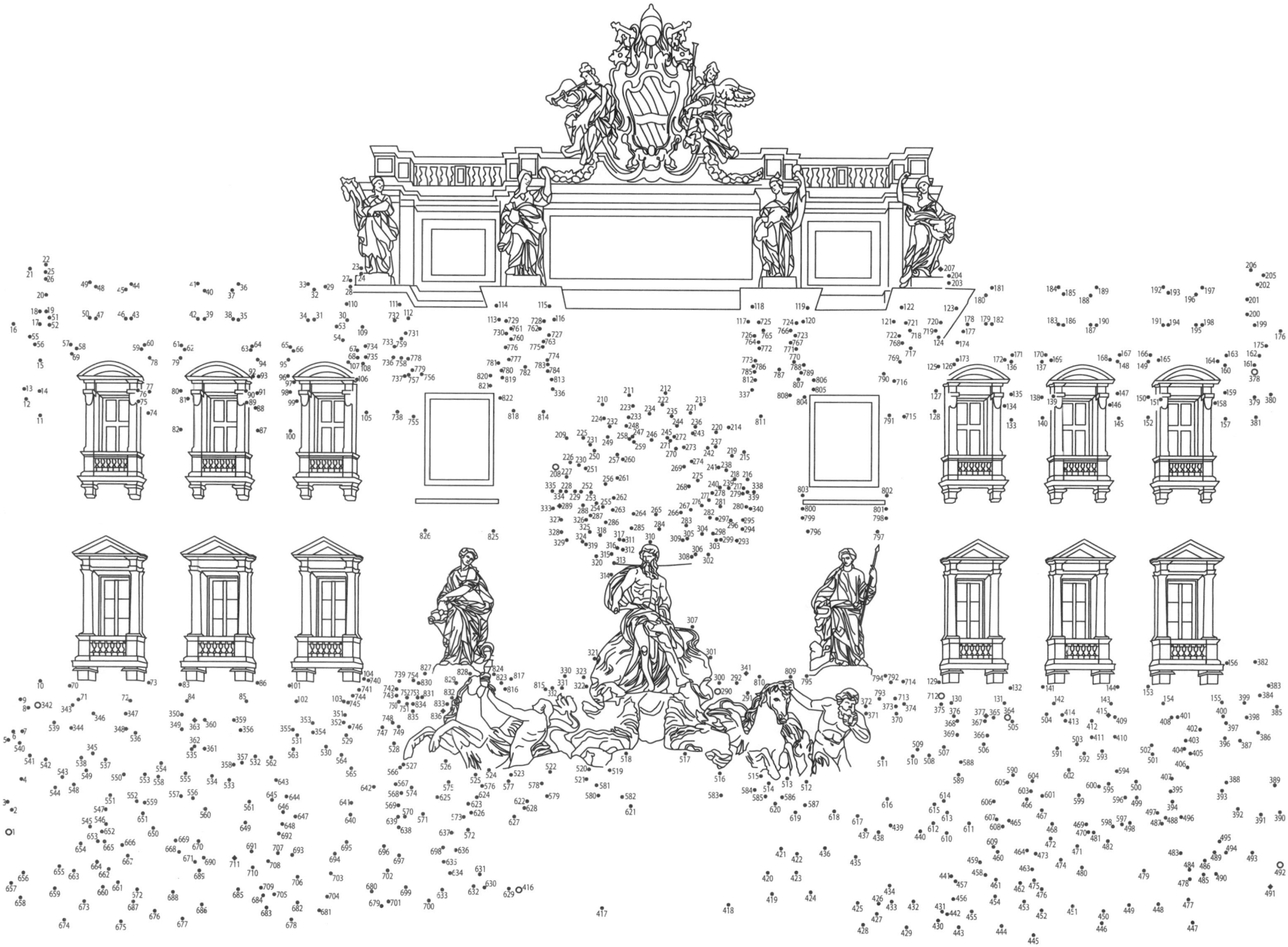

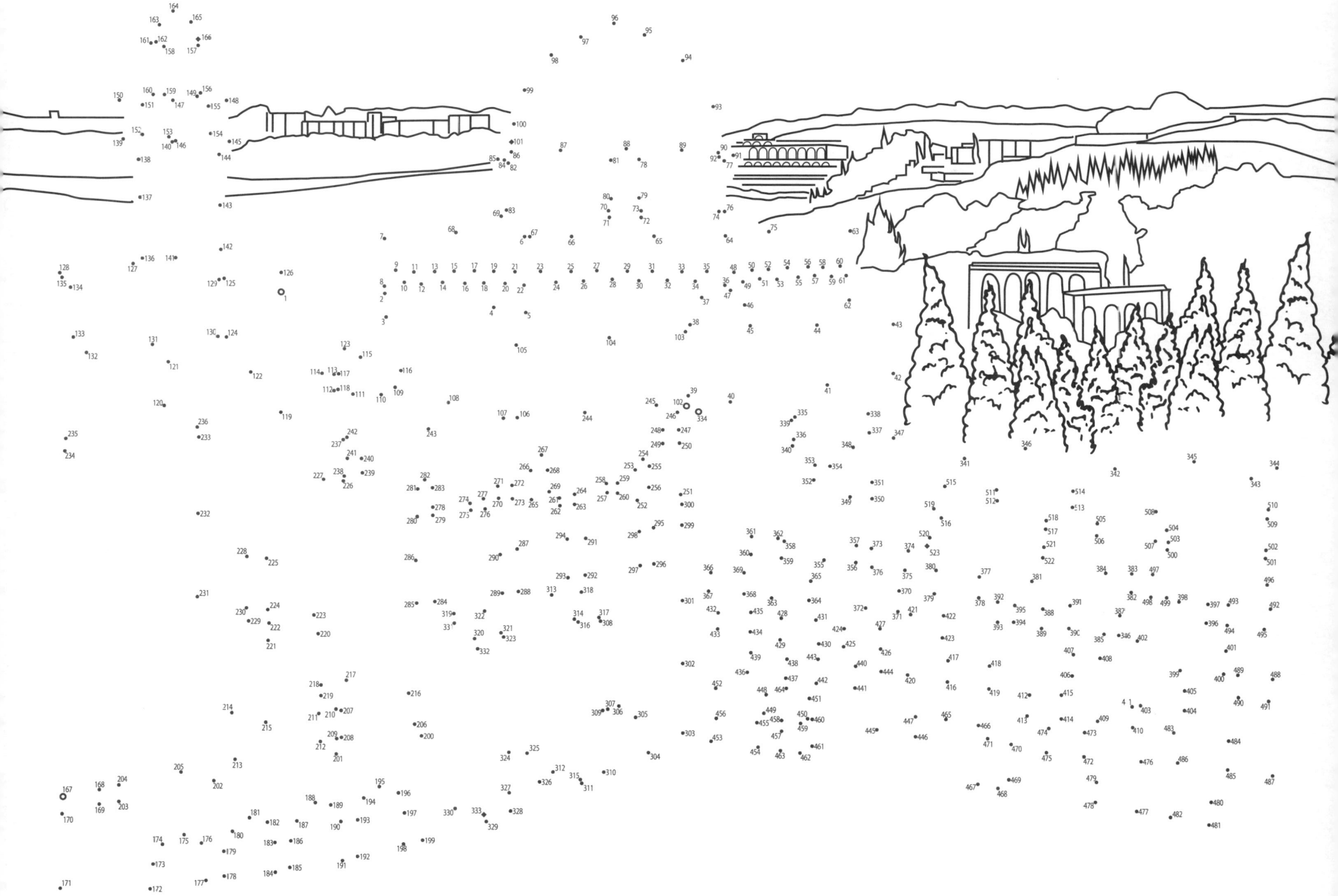

ANSWER KEY

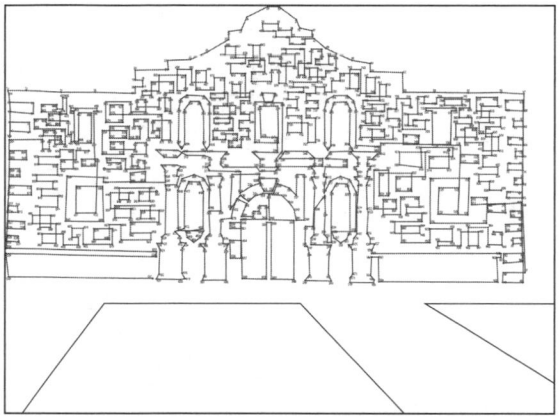

1. The Alamo - San Antonio, Texas, USA

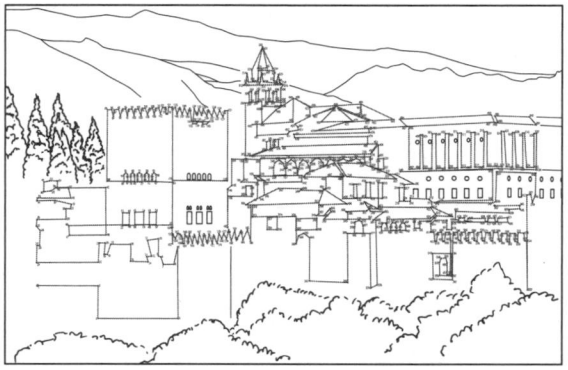

2. Alhambra - Granada, Spaint

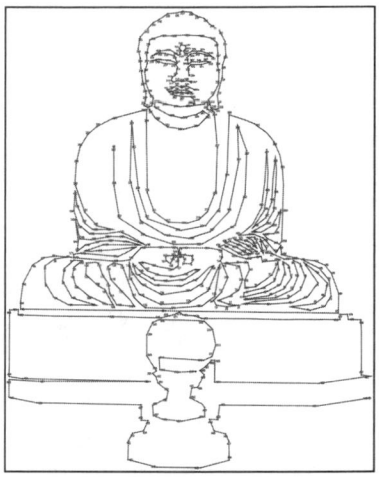

3. Amida Buddha - Kōtoku-in Temple, Kamakura, Japan

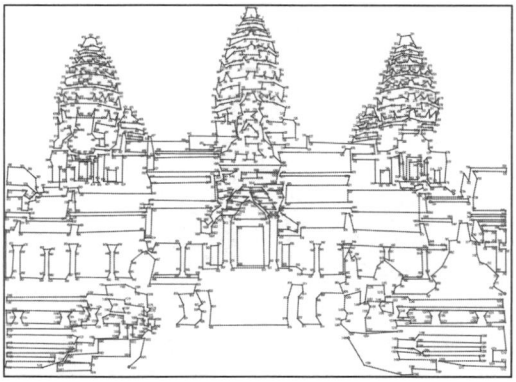

4. Angkor Wat - Angkor, Siem Reap Province, Cambodia

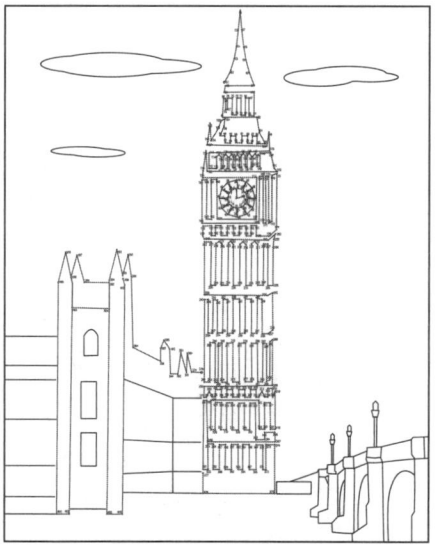

5. Big Ben (Elizabeth Tower) - London, United Kingdom

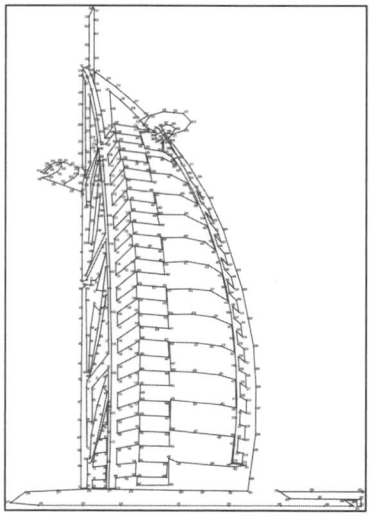

6. Burj Al Arab - Jumeirah, Dubai, United Arab Emirates

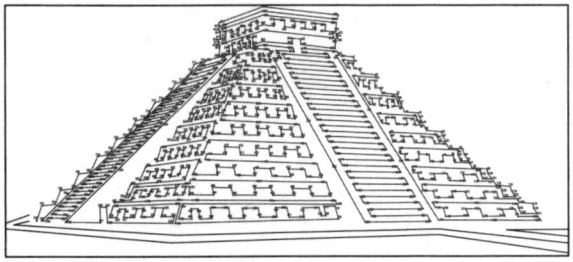

7. El Castillo, Chichen Itza - Chichen Itza, Mexico

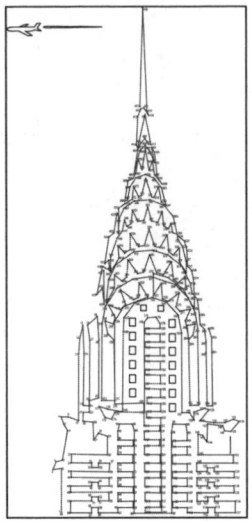

8. The Chrysler Building - New York City, New York, USA

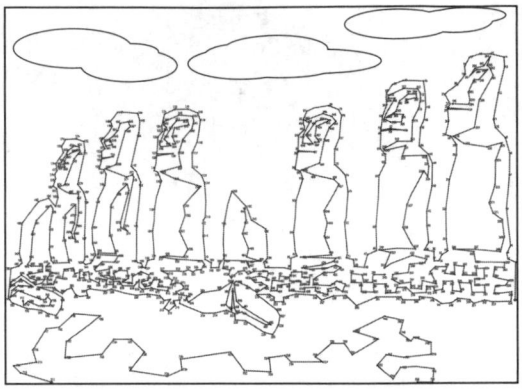

9. Moai - Ahu Akivi, Easter Island

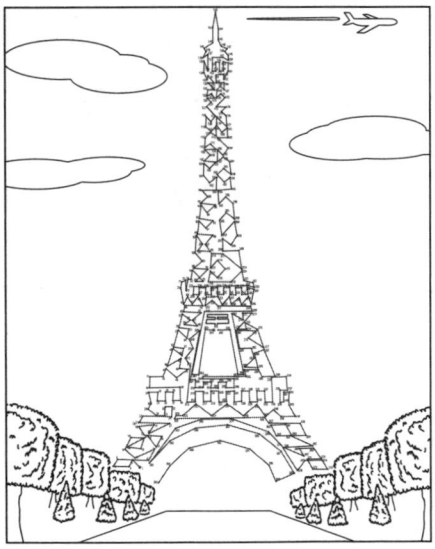

10. The Eiffel Tower - Paris, France

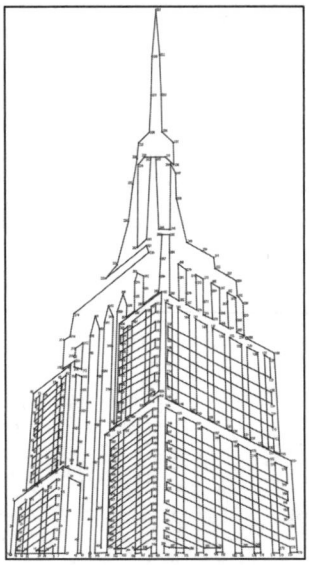

11. The Empire State Building - New York City, New York, USA

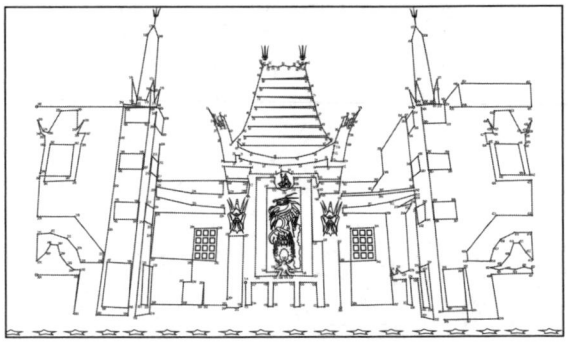

12. Grauman's Chinese Theatre - Hollywood, Los Angeles, California, USA

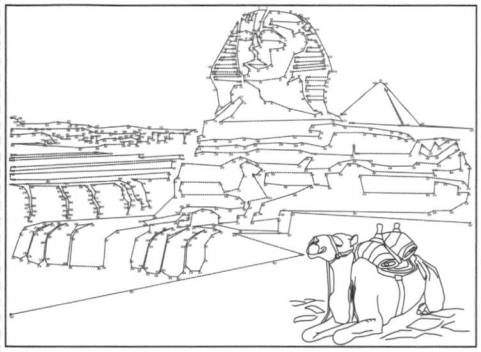

13. The Great Sphinx of Giza - Giza, Egypt

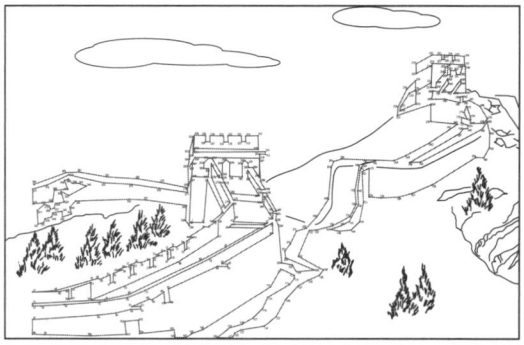

14. The Great Wall of China - China

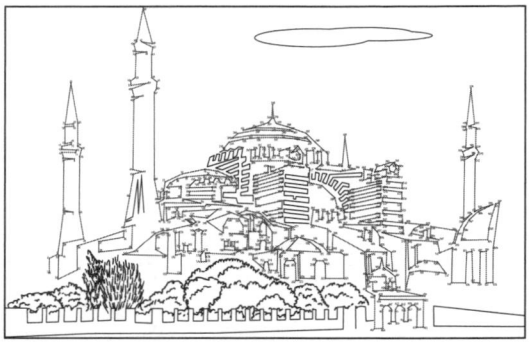

15. Hagia Sophia - Istanbul, Turkey

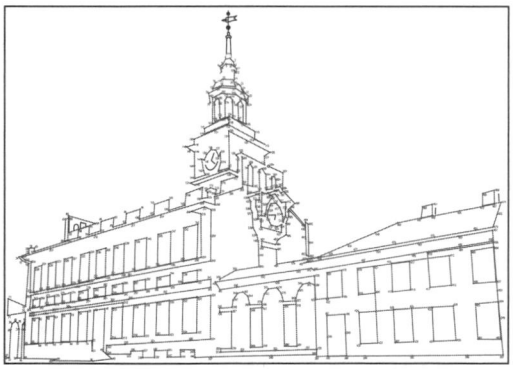

16. Independence Hall - Philadelphia, Pennsylvania, USA

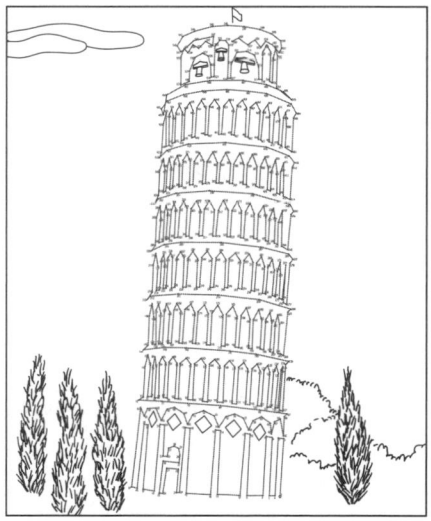

17. The Leaning Tower of Pisa - Pisa, Italy

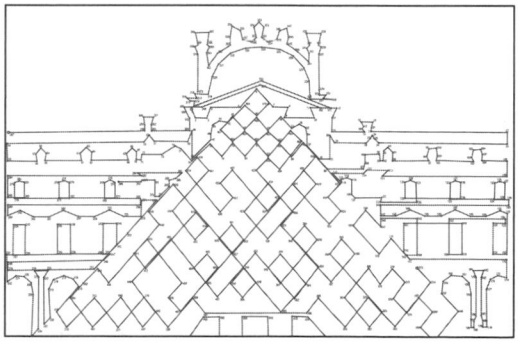

18. The Louvre Museum - Paris, France

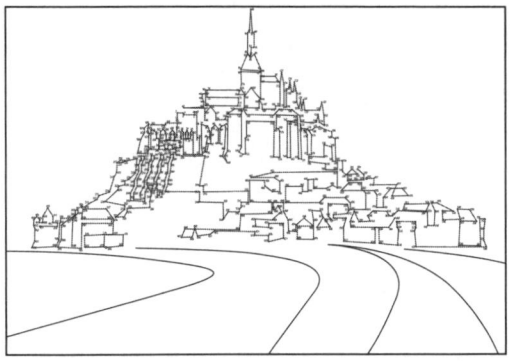

19. Le Mont-Saint-Michel - Normandy, France

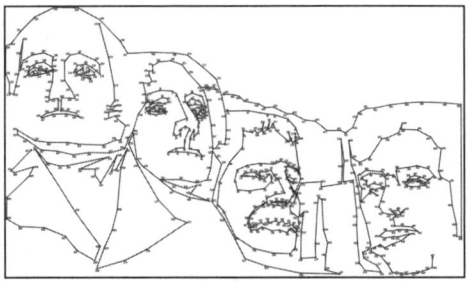

20. Mount Rushmore - Pennington County, South Dakota, USA

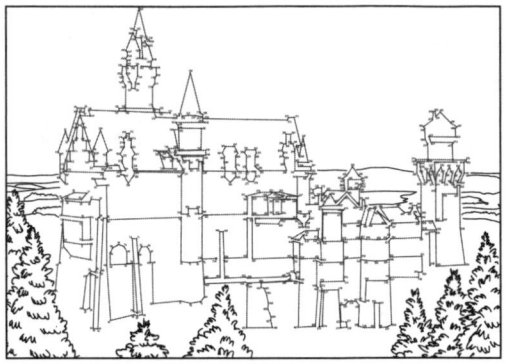

21. Neuschwanstein Castle - Hohenschwangau, Germany

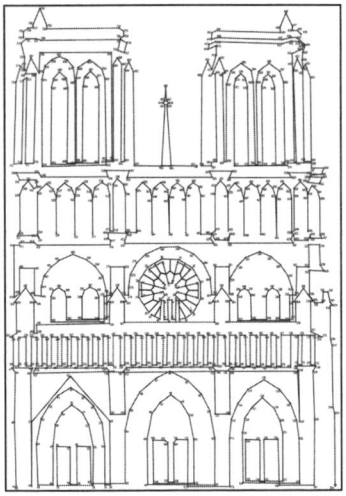

22. Notre-Dame Cathedral - Paris, France

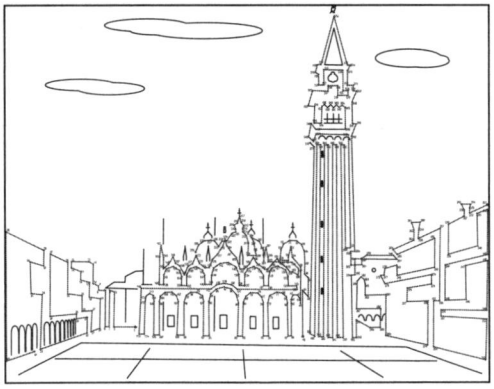

23. St Mark's Square - Venice, Italy

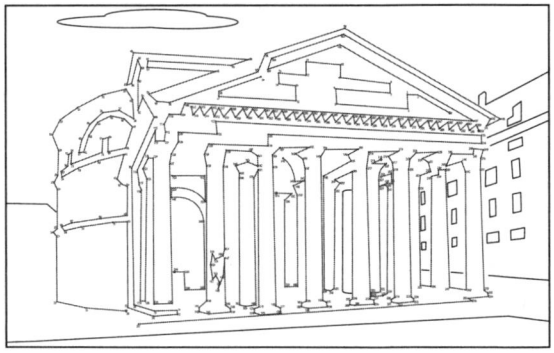

24. The Pantheon - Rome, Italy

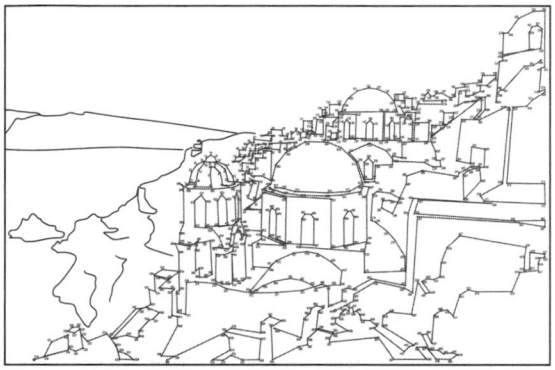

25. Oia - Santorini, Greece

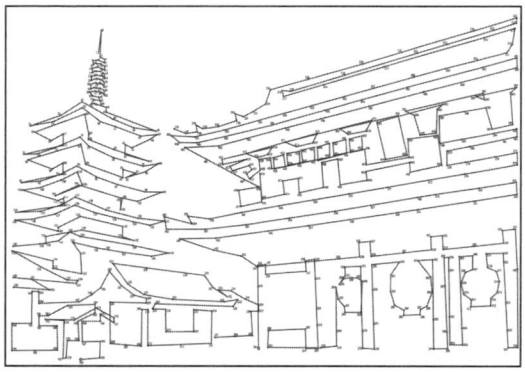

26. Sensō-ji Temple - Asakusa, Tokyo, Japan

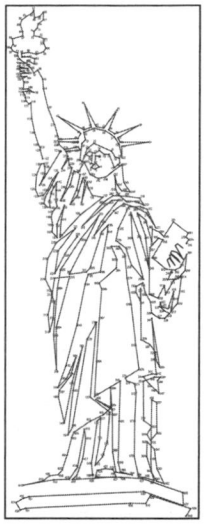

27. The Statue of Liberty - New York City, New York, USA

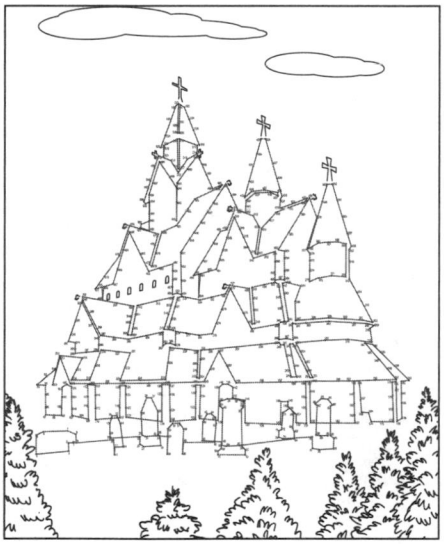

28. Urnes Stave Church - Ornes, Norway

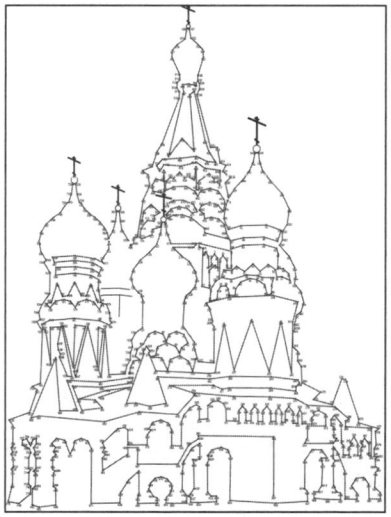

29. Saint Basil's Cathedral - Moscow, Russia

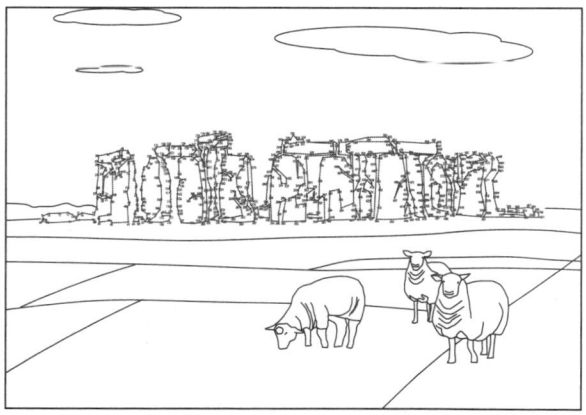

30. Stonehenge - Wiltshire, England

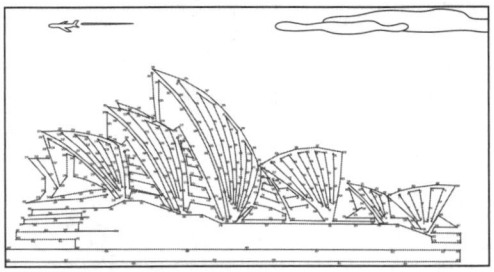

31. Sydney Opera House - Sydney, Australia

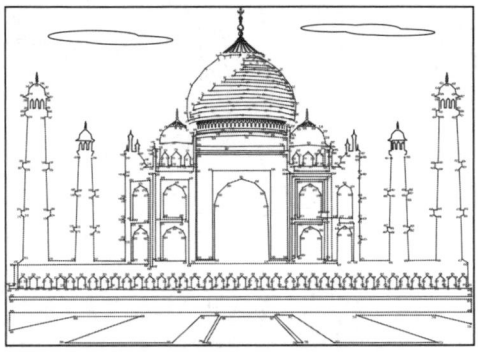

32. The Taj Mahal - Agra, India

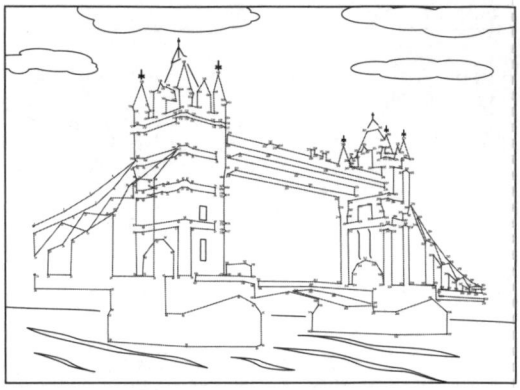

33. Tower Bridge - London, United Kingdom

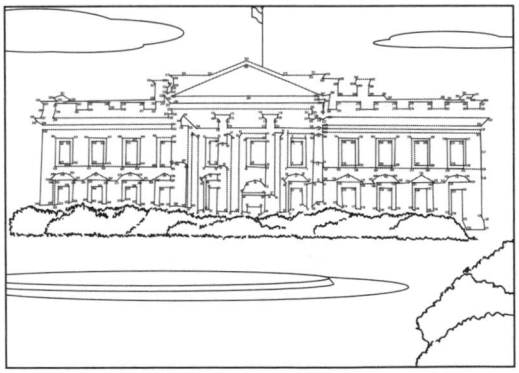

34. The White House - Washington, DC, USA

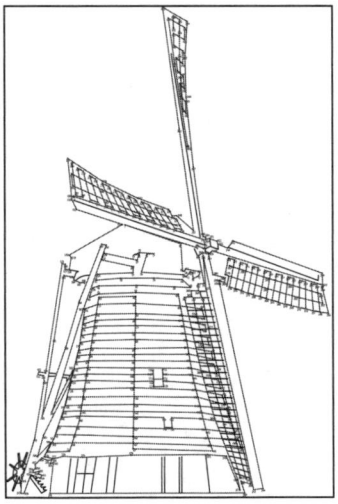

35. Windmills - Kinderdijk, Netherlands

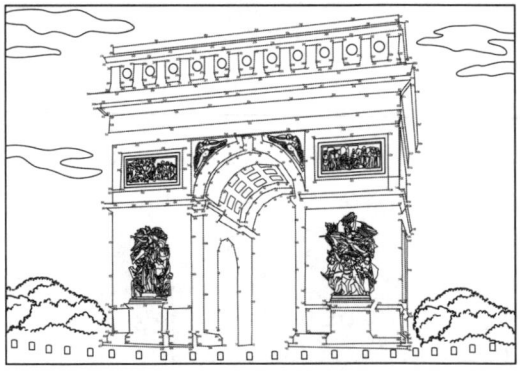

36. Arc de Triomphe - Paris, France

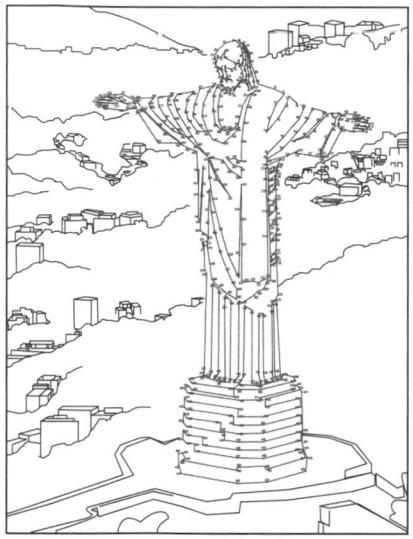

37. Christ the Redeemer -
Rio de Janeiro, Brazil

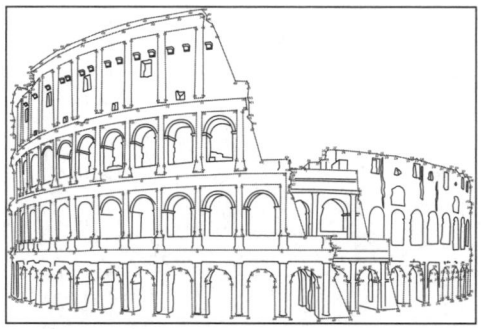

38. The Colosseum - Rome, Italy

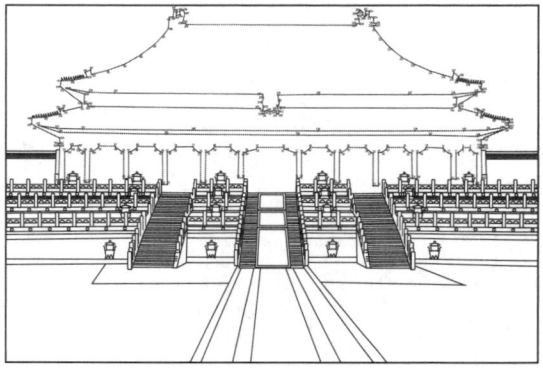

39. The Forbidden City - Beijing, China

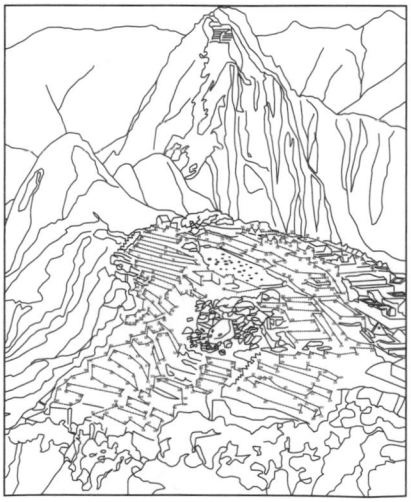

40. Machu Picchu -
Cuzco Region, Peru

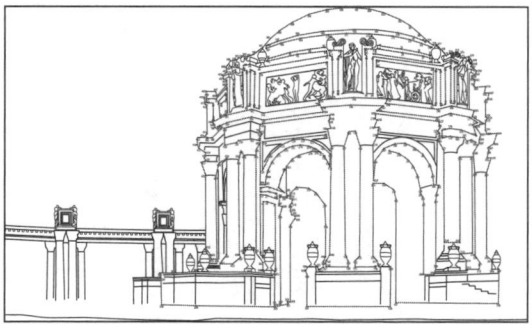

41. The Palace of Fine Arts -
San Francisco, California, USA

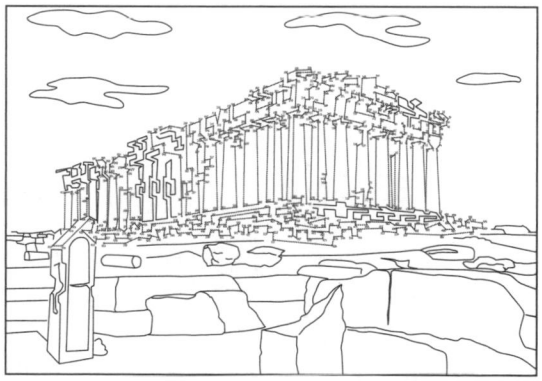

42. The Parthenon - Athens, Greece

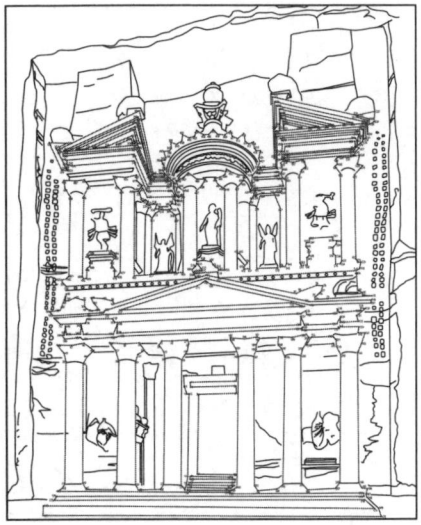

43. Al Khazneh - Petra, Jordan

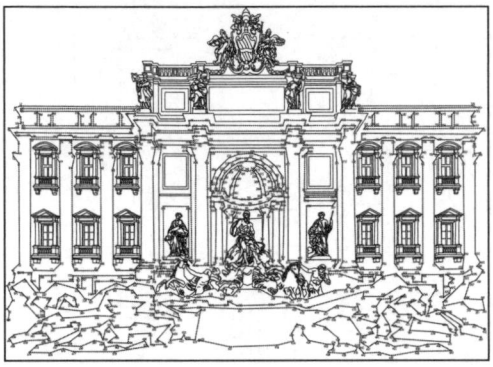

44. Trevi Fountain - Rome, Italy

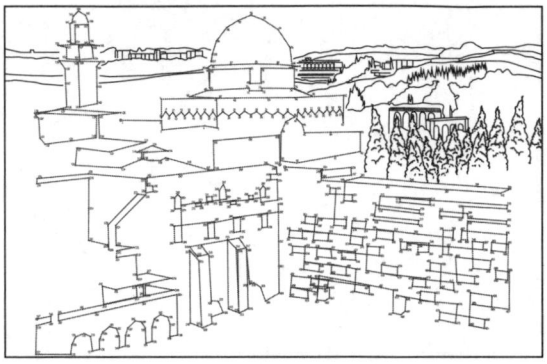

45. The Western Wall and The Dome of the Rock - Jerusalem